Advance Praise for *Time to Thank*

"This book provides a poignant road map of life's journey, illustrating how those who care deeply pour their everything into ensuring no one feels alone. Personally knowing Stanley, visiting each other's homes, and witnessing the devoted care from his family, alongside Steve's unwavering presence, has deeply influenced the memories and love for a father within this book. It promises to resonate with you, offering insight into a shared experience to which we can all relate."

—Woody Harrelson,
actor and playwright

"Steve Guttenberg has written an intensely personal story about his childhood and rise to fame as an actor in Hollywood. The journey is rich in detail and even intrigue, but mostly this beautiful memoir is a testament to the power of the love between a father and son."

—Holly Goldberg Sloan, *New York Times* bestselling author of *Counting by 7s*

"As a movie and Broadway star, Steve has always delivered. Now in his new book, *Time to Thank*, Steve reveals the most magnificent relationship he shared with his dad—the stories are heartwarming, hopeful, sometimes sad but always full of love. I'm confident Steve can also add bestselling author to his long, illustrious resume. Read this book! DON'T QUIT!"

—Jake Steinfeld, entrepreneur and fitness icon

"From the title alone, I was more than prepared to join Steve Guttenberg on his vivid journey, as he chronicles the daily rigors of caring for a beloved parent at the end of his life. What I hadn't expected, however, was a love story—and such a thoroughly touching one at that. From the first page to the last, Guttenberg draws for us a remarkable map of how a rebellious and adventurous boy turned into a spectacular and loving man, and how that transformation brought such richness into both men's lives. By anyone's standard, Steve's dad was a hero—principled, kind, a proud veteran, and a hardworking man who saw the good in everyone and brought goodness to all of his endeavors. But what *Time to Thank: Caregiving for My Hero* teaches us most preciously is how all that decency can be so passionately paid back—and forward. How proud Mr. Guttenberg would be to see that his loyal and devoted son is, in the end, so triumphantly a chip off the ol' block."

—Marlo Thomas, actor,
producer, and author

Time *to* Thank

To Carli!

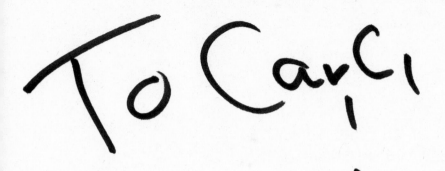

Time *to* Thank

STEVE GUTTENBERG

Post Hill
PRESS

A POST HILL PRESS BOOK
ISBN: 979-8-88845-146-5
ISBN (eBook): 979-8-88845-147-2

Time to Thank:
Caregiving for My Hero
© 2024 by Steve Guttenberg
All Rights Reserved

Cover design by Jim Villaflores

Post Hill Press
New York • Nashville
posthillpress.com

Published in the United States of America
1 2 3 4 5 6 7 8 9 10

For Mom and Dad

The first man I ever saw, who held me close
and began to teach me the art of living.

Chapter ONE

M y father has kidney failure.

It's been building up for many years. He, like all of us, ignored the signs that health experts and his body shouted about. His doctors were more vocal; his body only discussed it in the numbers that appeared on his yearly physical—if it was yearly. And it caught up to him. And to us, his wife and three kids.

Tomorrow is my father's eighty-ninth birthday. There's added urgency to the four-hundred-mile drive I make each week: Los Angeles to Phoenix, straight on the 10 freeway, through the city, past the digital billboards, the new and old construction, to the first grains of desert sand. The plastic and concrete structures of Palm Springs beckon, but I stay committed until the 10 introduces the rubber of my front wheels to hotter pavement—a stretch of blacktop that leads to the desolate and solitary wilderness. A passerby might look at this as four hundred miles of nothing. To me, it has become everything.

Maybe you're like me, someone who loves and cares for aging parents. And maybe, like me, you're reluctant sometimes to remember that they aren't still the strong and vigorous people who brought you up. Who held you, bathed you, taught you to read the alphabet, ride a bike, write your name, confront a bully, face your fears, ask a girl or boy to a dance.

For me, the days are getting shorter, and time more precious. It's funny the way time masks itself when you're younger. Then you turn around, and you're not twenty anymore, and suddenly time is no longer infinite. It was a defining moment when I realized I wouldn't be here in perpetuity. Exhilarating: I want to do as much as I can to squeeze everything from life, knowing that it's too fast and nimble for my fingers to hold tight. And at the end of "time" is "me." Just me.

I believe G-d gives us spaces of time in life that can be filled with what is needed. And this time in my life is for me to give devotional attention to my parents: to embrace them, to repay them for all they've done for me.

When I leave the house at three a.m., my mission is to try not to wake my wife Emily and fool the dog into thinking I'm just getting up to pee.

If I'm able, I crawl into bed the night before at seven, trying to get as near to eight hours of shut-eye as I can. That usually means a nine o'clock tuck-in—if I'm lucky—and whatever hours of Zzzs I can get. It sure feels like something is wrong when you wake up at two thirty in the morning.

Inch by inch, I try my darnedest not to make the sheets rub together but fail to slither out unnoticed. Gracie, the family dog, has both of her Marty-Feldman-distanced Spaniel eyes open. She sleeps on my pillow, above my head. Yes, it's odd, but I haven't found a way to talk her out of it. She's a small batch of fur, and resting near my noggin gives her a safe feeling—when she's up there, me rolling over onto her isn't a possibility.

It's a contest: she's observing me, and I'm crawling across the carpet; both of us are trying to keep the other from knowing that we've seen them. We're both losing at this game. She knows I'm up, and I know she knows. And she's angry.

I rattle around the bathroom, using the glow of my iPhone to navigate. Where are my socks? Will this shirt be warm enough for the cold and damp California morning but cool enough for the blazing heat of the desert? I gather my dopp kit, dress in the closet, and attempt again to silently creep toward the bedroom door.

I almost make it there when I hit my toe against the doorstop.

Gracie starts to wail, waking my wife Emily, who sees no purpose in my driving so early but understands why I go. My father started dialysis about four months after our wedding. So, with the dog howling at the ceiling, I close the bedroom door behind me.

I half-fall down the stairs. I put on some Stan Smith sneakers, load my duffle bag into the car, and try to silently drift down the driveway without waking the neighbors. The windshield fogs up in the cold air. I try to remember the tricks about defrosting a car's windshield. I never can remember, so I wipe the glass with my sleeve. I'm left with a soaked arm to go with a cup of black coffee and whatever was in the fridge that I could steal.

So begins my drive. I can still hear Gracie howling, pissed off about my weekly sojourn, and that she isn't a part of it.

My father used to get up early for work.

It was 1966, and I was nine years old, living in Massapequa, Long Island. The newfangled digital clock next to my bed told me it was four thirty in the morning—two more hours to sleep—but I knew that my father was starting his day. I could hear his footsteps on the creaky emerald green shag carpeting that covers the stairs, even though he held the handrail to try to stay as quiet as he could. I snuck out of bed in time to hear him cursing out the radiator as the heat crackled its way out into the house.

"Damn you," he whispered to the radiator. "Be quiet—everyone is sleeping."

He said the same thing to the radiator every morning. It never listened.

I watched him from the landing as he set the coffee going before creeping back upstairs and into the shower. The house was so quiet that I could make out the sound of his razor scraping against his skin; he kept the tap off in the sink as he shaved, worried it would make too much noise. He tiptoed to his dresser, put on his socks and underwear, and gingerly removed his shirt, tie, and suit from the closet he shared with my mother. I crept back into my room.

He looked in on my sisters in the room next to mine and then looked in at me, still holding the hangers with his clothes for the day.

"I know you're up, Steven," he said. "You okay?"

"I'm okay," I said. He turned to leave. "Dad? Why are you up so early every day?"

"So I can feed my family. You'll see. One day, you'll creep around your house too."

I never thought it would be so I could come care for him.

Not a soul on the road at three a.m. on the west side of LA. There isn't even a bakery truck. No newspaper deliveries yet, and even the streetlights turn their heads at me in disbelief.

I am on my own.

Los Angeles to Phoenix. My car bends along the Pacific Coast Highway to the 10 freeway. The Pacific Ocean, that old pal of mine, disappears behind me. My coffee is warm, the steering wheel cold, and I try to sip the java without scalding myself. I've done that plenty of times before. There are stains all over the car to prove it.

My car pulls me like a magnet to Peoria, Arizona. To my father, Stanley Jerome Guttenberg, who waits for me. Our stories are getting more intertwined, like the vines of a money tree, holding on to each other for dear life. And that's what it is: dear life.

He does dialysis. The system takes every drop of blood from his body and circulates it through the complex mystery of a machine. It chills his blood to thirty-four degrees, filters out the toxins that his body can't handle anymore, and returns it to his veins through what's called a fistula. The technical term is "challenging his system," and it absolutely does.

I love this machine. I love every inch of Dr. Willem Kolff, the Dutch scientist who invented it. I love that every city, every town has these marvels. They keep the blood of millions clean—the blood that built countless lives, nurtured babies, taught kids how to ride their bikes, eat with utensils, talk, write, and think. But the blood I'm searching for, that I drive fifteen hours a week to find, is my father's.

The cleaning is a four-day-a-week ritual. It keeps him alive. Four hours per day. Four hundred miles per rubber tire. The number four has become my rhythm, the beat of which I now live. Now one of the purposes of my life.

My father used to watch me sleep in my bed, guarding me with his gaze. I now watch my father sleep during the circulation of his red energy, guarding him with my own gaze.

It's always cold during these early morning drives through California—a stark reminder that everything isn't as advertised. I'm a believer, an optimist of epic proportions; I can be fooled, on the surface at least. But it doesn't last long. The terrible part of getting older is knowing how the song ends and trying to keep it inside. Naivete has been a friend of mine for so long. But it gets thinner every year; I can't count on it anymore. I miss it. I miss the way it kept me blissfully unaware for so long. I miss my old pal ignorance.

When I first came to Hollywood, my parents gave me two weeks and $300. They believed that in my youthful endeavor, I could be trusted. Their hope for a measure of maturity meant that I could do what I dared to; my parents intended the cash for food and gasoline to shepherd me around Tinseltown.

I spent almost the whole shebang on photos of myself.

The third day of my sojourn, I waited at a bus stop on Second Street in Santa Monica. I was still glowing with innocence, believing in the dream of stardom. I was hoping for my own version of being discovered on a stool at the counter of the legendary Schwab's Drugstore on Sunset Boulevard. The sunshine, the sidewalks that looked like diamond inlaid, wall-to-wall carpet, and every car held the promise of someone who might discover me. A bright red Cadillac pulled up, and a man with blond hair and the darkest sunglasses I ever saw called out to me.

"You Gluberman?"

Close enough, I thought.

"Yes, that's me."

"Have you got the money?" His hands were covered in gold rings, and someone with even darker glasses sat next to him.

"Right here," I said, pulling out my wad of green. I still had the money clip my father gave me, on the promise I wouldn't lose it. I waved the cash like a flag on the Fourth of July.

"Are you nuts? Put that cash away! Hop in the back, and keep quiet."

I did just that, and the car sped away.

This was my photographer. Beneath me in the back seat, stacked up on the fake leather, were hundreds of stale, black-and-white headshots. Victims of his lens from days gone by. My hands caught a couple, and I took a look.

"Are my pictures going to look like this?" I said, holding up the faces brimming with charm.

"Gimme the two hundred. We'll start shooting at the McDonald's on the corner. And you'll like what you see, believe me."

I handed the cash to the man with the dark glasses in the passenger seat. He counted it like a machine and looked at me over his shoulder.

"I'm Mikey. I'll be doing your hair and makeup. Jesus, you are young. How old are you kid?"

I wondered if I should lie. "Seventeen, but I'll be eighteen in three months." I prayed they wouldn't kick me out for being underaged.

Jamie, the photographer, laughed.

"You'll age quickly youngster. This town puts lines on your face before you can change your shirt."

The car pulled into the fast-food parking lot. I was in a waitstaff uniform in two minutes and behind the counter in half that. Jamie's camera flashed so many times that I had trouble making it out the door. As I stumbled to the red boat, he grabbed me.

"Nah, let's do the headshots and be done with this."

I stood against the car and he clicked away. Suddenly he handed me a folded magazine with a naked lady on the cover.

"Here's my address. Come see me in three days. I'll have the proofs for you."

I looked at the scrawl on the margin.

"Does that say Laurel Canyon?"

"You can read, good boy."

The two hopped in the car and started to pull out. I chased them and slapped my hand on the hood.

"I thought I was supposed to get makeup," I said. "I didn't get any makeup."

"You don't need any color, 'Fresh Face.' But believe me, this town will eat your skin like an appetizer, and you'll need pounds of makeup later. Just appreciate your youth. See you in a few days."

And he was gone. My introduction to the business: it doesn't owe me anything.

I stood at a payphone on Santa Monica Boulevard 'til the night fell on me. I waited until eight o'clock to call my parents. The rates were cheaper at night, but the street was full of characters from a zombie movie. I thought if I opened the door to the booth I would be eaten alive.

My father answered, and my mother picked up the extension. I told them the extent of my first professional day.

"Steven, how do you know you'll get these pictures? You just gave him almost all the money you have."

"I'm okay, Dad—I have his address, and I'll get the proofs in three days."

"Stanley, I knew he shouldn't have gone out there." My mother was mad as hell and worried to her core.

There was silence.

"Dad?"

"You need to grow up, son, and you need to do it quickly."

The air turned cold, and the receiver felt sticky with something someone left on it. My quarter was about to run out. I was way too far from home. And way too young to be there.

I waited for the bus to come, and I could see the ocean between the strangers who circled my bench. The water in the dark looked like a familiar face, the only face I recognized.

The city of Santa Monica has the look of old Brooklyn: short buildings clumped together. The people are in their beds now, some dreaming, some waiting to awaken, some sitting up and thinking in the middle of the night. Ruminating. That dreaded rumination.

I can't avoid it when I'm on the road. Think about all the thoughts you have during an active day, when there are other things to distract you. Then put yourself alone for six or seven hours doing one task. And thinking. Gobs of time to think.

Have I done right in my life? When I was younger, the dream was still a dream, and anything was possible. But now I feel like I'm waking up to some stirring. It feels like life is pushing me up against a wall, but at the same time it feels like I'm being held in someone's warm arms. I think about my dad: married at twenty-six, working like a dog for his family, not taking a vacation for fourteen relentless years with three small children in the house. He was not a man of hobbies or bars; he wanted to come home after he was done with work to be with his family. He would eat all the leftovers in the fridge, consuming what we didn't, feeding himself with what the family put aside. And he made us shine. Sometimes I feel like I'm not a grain of sand compared to all that.

When we humans agree to our annual physical, we are laden down with charts and numbers. We peruse the figures to see if the numbers land between the appointed boundaries. Do we actually know what any of this means? Not a chance. But the ones that are circled catch our eyes.

It's creatinine levels that are important to renal patients. And you don't even know you're a kidney client until those numbers are circled.

Years ago, my father's internist suggested we visit a specialist. We didn't listen. And slowly, year after year, my father's creatinine went further up the scale. He felt fine, but eventually the numbers got so high that we had to visit a renal clinic. My father is a veteran of the Korean War—he's proud of his service as a paratrooper in the Eighty-Second Airborne, his Ranger training infused from his toes to his temples. So the VA was where we went to seek out kidney expertise.

His kidneys were loaded with cysts. We met with a doctor, Dr. Robey. That first meeting was like a carnival. A glorious hour and a half of my father telling his favorite stories: from the Army, from his business—stories that gave him comfort and allowed him to regale in his victories. I joined in, telling a few stories of my own. But I knew I was telling stories for a different reason—to avoid the reality of the meeting, why we were really there, and what it meant for my dad.

Dr. Robey—patient saint that she is—laughed at our stories and spoke in awed tones about the determination my father had clearly shown his entire life. We enjoyed having a new set of ears to listen to us. But at the same time, she was preparing us. It was going to be a new kind of life, what lay ahead. Her suggestion: Dad does dialysis three days a week.

Even with what we already knew heading into the meeting, it was a shock. My mom's face fell; I could see how greatly she was affected. The dialysis was going to become a part of his life—and his family's. We were going to build our lives around Dad's schedule. All his food had to change. And, even more importantly, we had to carefully monitor his fluid intake—the dialysis would not only filter the toxins from his blood but also help remove the fluids that were building up in his left lung.

The family had to commit. If Dad has dialysis, we all do.

Once the start date for dialysis was set, we spent the days counting down to it, confronting everything we still didn't know about what was to come. What's down there in the river that we know not of? Is it easy to swim? The waiting was painful. My father held it in, but what were we in for? Not until they pierce your skin for the first time do you know what dialysis is like. Not until you experience your parent having a health crisis do you know what real fear is. And it comes out of nowhere.

It was 2005. I was having lunch in the Village with my friend Paul Riccio. Paulie is a foodie exemplar. I was having such a good time, watching as he delivered a sermon on every bite; we ate like food critics.

I called my folks, as I usually did a few times a day, to see what was up.

My father answered and could only say "no."

"Dad?"

"No."

"Dad, are you okay?"

"No."

My mother picks up the extension. "Stanley, what do you mean, 'no'?"

"No?"

"Stanley! What the hell is wrong with you?"

Already gone from the table, I switched into my Prius and flew down the 495 to Massapequa and onto Wyoming Avenue. The sun was just setting when I got to my parents' house, and my father was in his bed. He couldn't talk—he could only say "no." I begged him to get out of bed—to walk, to move. My brother-in-law Bob told me Dad should get to the ER. I only managed to get him to the downstairs den, knowing all the while we would have to go to the hospital.

But Dad didn't want to leave the house.

The thoughts of your parent having an episode are like spikes on the inside of your cranium. This was the first chink in my dad's armor—at least the first I ever saw. He was always the one who stood at the vanguard, the first to take a shot, and he would stand unflinching. To see him falter was like getting hit by a load of bricks. I don't think I blinked for a full day. *This isn't how my father is. He's not out of control. He's not this person.* But then I looked and that was my father.

"Dad, please come in the car."

"No."

I couldn't get him to come with me to the hospital. My sister, my mother, my brother-in-law watched with the same pain I had. My best friend, Joe, walked into the house and didn't say a word, which, if you know Joe, is impossible.

We didn't want to call 911. I didn't want to do that to him. I knew how he would feel, the embarrassment. So he sat on the couch in his jogging suit, huddled under a blanket.

He didn't want to go to the hospital. What could I do? Nothing would move him. I thought fast.

"Dad," I said. "I have to go to the hospital."

"What?"

"I think I'm having a heart attack. Will you go with me to the hospital?"

And so, my father got up and went in the car with me. He couldn't be moved, not one inch, when he was the one who needed to go to the hospital. But when I told him it was for me, that I needed him to help me, his parental juices started to rise into his body, through those veins and capillaries to his head and his heart. For my son, I'll do anything. That's a parent.

We drove to the ER. Dad knew something was up, especially when the nurses started to tend to him. We were swept into an examination room. My father started to have a panic attack. He forced himself into a corner, which he thought was a door, and scratched at the walls, screaming to go back home, to his bed, to safety.

Is this, Plainview Hospital, the correct hospital for my father? Do they have the equipment we need? The world was going two hundred miles per hour. My eyes saw things speeding by, then slowing, when it came to Dad.

Noises from the next room: the ER floor, the machines, the announcements over the loudspeakers. The noise here: my heart pounding two hundred beats per minute.

They say it's surreal. But that wasn't my experience. Surreal has to do with art, with moments of bliss. This was stark raving reality.

My father was huddled in a corner, trying to reason with us. His eyes, no longer black, were red and wider than I'd ever seen.

My mom and sister are both strong women. They projected calm and presence, but I could tell they were frightened—it was beyond anything I've ever seen in their eyes. I held my father as he tried to get out of the room, running from corner to corner. He was powerful, and I tell you, holding your father is a difficult thing. It makes you aware that you are interfering with someone who interfered with you. He was the one who protected me. He watched for my welfare. He took my hand every time I faltered and told me everything would be alright. He sat quietly with me when all I needed was to know someone was there. And now it was me holding him.

I did just that. I told him everything was going to be alright. That we had to behave, to calm down, to breathe deeply. Doctors came into the room, and each seriously told us different plans and points of view. And while my father was flipping out, the rest of us—my

12

mother, my sister, Joe, and I—were trying to fit ten thousand pounds of information into a thimble.

It's just another reminder about life. When it's slow, it's molasses. When a crisis walks in, the world spins faster, and everything comes at you. Life has balance until it doesn't. Where did it go?

I watched my poor father get strapped into a contraption like a lion who has gotten caught in a net. The humiliation: he didn't know what was happening, or why he was there. The doctors didn't have the correct diagnostic machines in the hospital. The shame I felt, telling my father what to do. It was almost disrespect. But I continued protecting him, watching for his welfare. I took his hand and whispered that everything was going to be alright.

"Dad, I am here, and I am not going anywhere. We all are. I won't ever leave you alone."

They took my dad for an MRI—I went with him and kept my promise. I couldn't take my eyes off him. My father was strapped into a bed, the black bands keeping him from his freedom. I'm not sure if he heard us as we talked about what we were going to do. Our faces flush with emotion, we talked, not knowing what was happening with Dad and what to do. And he was right there next to us, his eyes wide, staring at the ceiling with confusion.

Night came, and my father was still strapped down, now with thick, protective mittens on his hands so he wouldn't hurt himself. A prisoner of this dramatic inconvenience. My family went home to get some rest. I slept on the floor at first, then a straight-backed chair. We were in a glass room, closed in with 360 degrees of observation. I laid my head on his sheets and waited for the morning. Maybe Dad would awaken, and he would be better. This was the hope bestowed upon us by the medical experts who still didn't know what to do for him. I prayed all night.

I woke up around five a.m., the room dreamlike around me for the first few moments of consciousness. Nurse after nurse swept in and out. The doctors started to talk outside the glass. I looked up, and my father was awake. Like a he-man Dorothy at the end of *The Wizard of Oz,* he was smiling. He was himself.

A nurse came into the room with a whisper. The MRI showed it was a TIA.

I just looked at her, bleary-eyed, not knowing what she meant.

"It's a small stroke, but it will have no lasting effect. He can go home in a few hours."

The moment you see a loved one come out of the fray, it takes a nanosecond to recognize it. But a nanosecond can be a long time. You're waiting for your eyes to tell your brain: he's alright. You know, but you don't want to know, that this is another calm before more storms to come in life.

He took my hand in his and asked, "Are you alright, Steven? You have a worried look on your face. I promise you, whatever it is, it'll be alright."

This is what my father did for me, every day of my life. When I got in trouble—and it was often: landing in jail, losing a girlfriend, getting fired from a job, being turned down for a role—he was at my side. Not with a roar, but a gentle hum. He always promised me it would be alright, no matter what happened.

It was summer 1963 in Flushing, Queens. The hydrant was open and everyone was running through it. On hot days, the kids—and parents for that matter—came from miles around. The cool water bursting from the fire hydrant creates not only puddles but also sheer delight, blossoms of happiness, and laughter for no reason other than glee. It's an honest moment. I see it like a photograph in my mind: a kid was laughing with me, his mouth open wide and his eyes full of jewels. It was raining diamonds.

My father called me in; it was time for supper. I was soaked, and we both walked into the elevator. It opened to the smell of food; every apartment was cooking—Indian, Italian, and in our apartment, Continental.

My mother hurried me into the bedroom between taking the veggies out of the oven. She pulled my shirt and pants off and told my dad to put dry clothes on me. Maybe pajamas. Dad looked at my arm; there was a pimple that was infected by a ring of beige-looking ooze. He pointed to something else.

"Steven, did you notice this?"

It was a red line, snaking up my arm, over my shoulder, and on its way to my heart. How did my dad know to look for it? I don't know, but he knew, and once he saw it, he jumped into action.

"Ann!" he called to my mother. "I'll watch Judi. You need to take Steve to Booth Memorial. He's got an infection making its way to his heart. If it gets there, he's dead."

My mother and I ran onto the nearest bus. She pulled me by my good arm up the steps to the grand hospital of Queens. By the time I was lying on a table, they lanced it. I probably spent a half hour in the waiting room bathroom, scared out of my mind, as my mother asked my father if they should open my arm up. I remember screaming; it's kind of funny to me now. Here's the shot: all black at first, and then the camera rises up out of my mouth to show me—this skinny wire of acid, all mouth and teeth, screaming my head off—before continuing up to a bird's-eye view of the operating theater.

When we got back from the hospital—another bus ride—my father held me in his arms.

"You're going to be alright, Steven."

This period of my life has caught me by surprise. I never planned for it. And I've always thought ahead, even down to my younger self thinking that my older self would need help. I put away for the future, saving mementos, photos, accolades, and books that brought me memories. Never did I think my time would be so devoted to my parents' quality of life. It's who I have become.

Speaking of that former me, I did get those headshots, after all. My godfather, Michael Bell, an old Brooklyn neighborhood friend of my parents, gave me his Pacer, an ugly as hell car, to drive through the machinations of Hollywood. It was an odd-looking spacecraft; very few were on the road. I drove up and down Laurel Canyon Boulevard, looking for the hidden address. It took two hours and gallons of precious gasoline, but I found it.

Mikey's head leaned out the second-story window of a house covered in red bougainvillea.

"Is that a Pacer? I didn't think they were legal. Doesn't it blow up if you hit it in the back?"

"I think that's a Corvair," I said. My eyes were straining against the sun coming from the east.

"Geez, I think you're wrong; it could blow. Mind parking it down the street?"

I did and then hiked a half mile back to the house.

"Come on in. Don't mind the dogs."

Two Rottweilers were growling behind a makeshift gate in the kitchen. He led me to a dark and musty room and shoved a magnifying glass in my hand.

"These are the ones we chose. These two."

I looked at them and thought they were lousy.

"Can I have these other two?"

Mikey frowned and sighed.

"You look like a dork in those. But sure. You know everything, huh, kid?"

Screw him, I thought.

"I know you didn't do any makeup on me."

"We'll call you when the photos are ready. How many do you want?"

"How much are they?"

"More than you can afford. Better have them printed in Pacoima, kid."

"Okay, where's that?"

"It's near where your ass is. Now get outta here, punk."

For a year and a half, I thought Pacoima was near a town called "Yourassis." Welcome to Hollyweird.

So I had the photos. And the other thing I managed to get, in those early days in LA, was my very own office at Paramount Studios.

I was staying out 'til all hours, looking for something—anything—that would get me into the business. The streets of Hollywood were a badass place after midnight, but that's when the action started. I didn't have much cash left, but what I did have was a mouth that went faster than a locomotive. So, I talked. I talked my way into clubs, into bars, into private house parties in the Hollywood Hills.

I even managed to talk my way right through the gates of Paramount.

But I didn't stop there. Once I was in, I found a deserted building: the Lucille Ball makeup building. I proceeded to clip a desk, chairs, and even a spliced telephone from the stage across the way. I set up my own office with ten days left to become a movie star. Long distance phone calls were suddenly no problem: I just asked the studio operator for an outside line.

"Dad!" I said. "I got an office! An office in a studio!"

"Steven, what are you talking about? What are you going to pay rent with? We gave you three hundred dollars for two weeks; you can't spend it all on rent."

"I got it for free. I snuck in! I commandeered it."

"Steven, I'm going to tell you this just once: that office is not yours. If you get caught, you'll never live it down."

"I won't get caught. I'm going to make you proud of me. I'm going to become someone."

"The thing is, you already are someone. Remember that. You are my son, and you'll always be everything to me. Is this show business really what you want?"

"Yes, Dad. I can do it. I want it with all my heart."

"Then go get what you want. Know your mother and I are always here for you. And know we love you, and we worry about you."

I never did get caught. And I got what I wanted. Though that part took a little longer.

Dad taught me that some days were good and to appreciate them. Some days there were lessons to be learned and to treasure just as much.

Dad loved to have coffee at the kitchen table—lunch or dinner—and talk with people. The art of conversation. I appreciate more today than ever before how my parents would have people over for "coffee and cake" every other night. Not late, but such an event to me.

Chapter TWO

My car pushes through a tunnel. I'm heading towards desert now. The sand blows through peach-hued buildings; the billboards all still shilling for something or another in show biz. There's William Shatner, selling Priceline. He's almost ninety and still at it, but he's not on dialysis. Why is my dad? Why is he getting older and these guys are still out there making commercials and movies?

I know he's had a good life. I know others haven't been as lucky as I have. But it's still not enough for this son.

No time to question it now, though. Just drive.

Everyone out here knows this road as the Santa Monica Freeway. But its true name, the one on its birth certificate, is the 10. And once I'm on it, all I have to do is drive straight for four hundred miles.

In the dark of my car, settling into the drive, I start to listen to the sermon—the cacophony of voices that come to me each time I make this trip. They're a reminder of what I did and didn't do in my life and a reminder, too, of what I have to do now. This drive is a battleground made of concrete and blacktop, and every time I have to win. To get to Arizona. To get to my father.

Once it became clear that my dad needed dialysis, we had two options for getting his body ready. The first was to have a port—basically a plastic cap that can be unscrewed to allow the transfer of blood to and from the artificial kidney. It's a handy option, but it has to be kept meticulously clean and safe from outside infections since it's a direct stretch of roadway to the bloodstream. The other, more difficult, option was to have what's called a fistula installed. In this procedure, the surgeon bundles together a few veins and melds them together to the artery into one mega, super vein—ten times the size of a normal vein. It bulges out of the arm like a python that's just had a meal. It's a miracle what modern medicine has built.

We chose the fistula—my dad was a weightlifter, and so the healthy veins just made sense, instead of putting a plastic circle in the middle of his chest. The surgery needed to be done six months before the start of dialysis. We all descended on the Mayo Clinic, the five of us—Mom and Dad, Susan, Emily and me—sitting in the waiting room like we were all scheduled for surgery. We disguised the worry on our faces as excitement, telling ourselves that we were doing our duty, getting things under control. My dad kept shaking his head in disbelief—how was this happening to him?

Installing the fistula involved a series of several operations. Day after day, the veins were monitored to make sure they were growing. Even then, it didn't feel real. Maybe there was still a way we could avoid the blood cleaning. Maybe this would all just go away. The months went on, and the fistula started to grow. We watched my father's arm take on the look of a bodybuilder—except that most of his forearm was this bulging, pulsating python of a fistula. They call that pulse a "thrill," pumping with every beat of his heart.

The first time I saw it, I thought of Tackapausha Pond out on Long Island, where I used to hold frogs in my hands along the banks. The way their hearts beat before I released them back into the water. Their fear building. Their hearts racing. And how I knew that pulse would slow back to their regular pace once they were returned to their homes. Their thrill would slow.

I knew what that felt like. How good it could feel to leave somewhere and go back home.

I had spent a year in an apartment in Westwood, LA, after I first moved to Hollywood. I used those head shots, and that office, to try and chase stardom. I actually bagged a few keepers. I shot twenty commercials and industrial films. I was the lead of a teen comedy opposite one of my dad's favorite actors, Phil Silvers. I costarred in a highly regarded movie of the week and even had a pilot for a TV series.

But the loneliness was unbearable for me. My parents had let me leave home three days after graduating from high school. It was what I said I wanted to do, but frankly I was just too young— seventeen!—to be ripped from authentic love and dumped in the middle of the Hollywood jungle. The most emotionally stunted and transactional city on the planet. The flesh business. A place where actors get bounced around. You have to have the bearings for it, and I didn't. You need a guide in these waters, and I was alone in my boat. For all my ambition—and I had lots of it—eventually the stark reality of friendships built solely on professional activity, the value systems with rubber boundaries, and the sheer loneliness of it all got to me.

I went and spoke to my agents, packed up my apartment, and moved back to the East Coast. I enrolled at Albany State University.

After Hollywood, college felt like a vacation from the real world. A magnificent place to hide out. I loved it. All I had to do was study, party, and sleep. The parade of casting, that relentless competition that had been my life for the last year, was over for me. I'd had enough.

And then, one morning, my roommate pulled me out of bed.

"Your dad's on the phone," he said. "Does he have to call at six a.m.?"

I went over and answered.

"Steven," my dad said. "The phone just rang and rang. I thought you said your suitemates were up before the sun rises."

23

"Dad, I said they get *in* at six a.m."

"Are you kidding me?"

"Sometimes," I said. "They're college freshmen."

What happened was that my agent had found me again. He had an appointment for me to meet about a movie, *The Boys from Brazil*, starring Gregory Peck and Laurence Olivier. It was bigger than anything I'd been a part of during my year in Tinseltown. I was keeping to my guns as long as I could. I was sure that I was never going back to Hollywood. Never.

"Steven," my dad said. "Go down there. Take the bus to Port Authority and see what the director and producers have in mind. You can always say no."

My father was a great believer in the idea that "if you don't go, you don't know."

I went to the audition. I got to the city after a four-hour trek from upstate and walked into the producers' circle office. I breezed in, sure that I wasn't going to do it even if I got offered the role of the young Jewish Defense League kid. The door opened, and there was the director, Frank Schaffner, and the producer, Marty Richards. Both of them were smooth as silk—the way they talked, the way they carried themselves, both of them intelligent and elegant. They even seemed authentic about their enthusiasm for my education and vowed to provide a tutor if I got the role. I pulled out the pages I'd memorized and read the scenes with a crafty acting coach named Milton. He was their tuner, the guy who could suss out talent in the way he read and how he could steer the energy of the scene to measure the abilities of the thespian opposite him. He took me around the course, and I held my own.

The audition was over—a quick and superficial thank-you, the same I'd heard at dozens of auditions before—and I was out. Back to Port Authority, and four more hours on the bus back up to Albany. It felt good to return to someplace where no one was a film actor, director, or producer—to be surrounded by college kids and professors. The town was the capital of New York—but no glamour there, unless you count the state majority leader visiting a high school science competition.

I was out. I'd done the audition and the phone didn't ring. I was free.

"You never know, Steven," my dad said on one of his regular morning calls. "They might call at any time. But you know your mother and I just want you to be happy. It doesn't matter what you do—just be happy."

I knew my father truly meant it. So I went back to being a student: going to classes late, studying 'til the wee hours, and partying 'til the sun rose.

Until the phone rang again. My roommate Danny, who loved movies, girls, and physics, answered.

"Guttenberg, someone on the phone, long distance."

I grabbed the shared phone. It was my agent, Arnold. Oh no, I thought.

"They want you," he said. "They'll get you a tutor and everything. You're going to Lisbon in a month. Get ready."

"Arnold, I haven't said yes yet."

"Oh, you'll say yes."

I took another bus down to New York and then another out to Massapequa. I surprised my family with the news, and they couldn't have been more excited about the prospect of my going overseas for the first time. But I wasn't so sure.

So I went into my parents' room, sat at the foot of their bed, and talked it over. I just didn't want this kind of inconsistent life: living all over the world without a real home, the loneliness, the anxiety that came from a freelance profession like acting. We stayed up until two in the morning talking about it. My parents were pure as could be in their desire for me to live a full, richly embroidered life, with love as the pinnacle.

"Steven, your father and I will be behind you, whatever you do," my mother said. "Just do what you want and be strong."

After we were done talking, I went to bed in my old bedroom and stared at the model plane hanging down from the ceiling. I looked out the window of our split-level to the house across the way, where another normal and loving family lived. The sky that night was full of stars.

I woke up the next morning with my dad sitting at the foot of my bed.

"Anything, Steven?"

"I want to do it, Dad."

"Good choice. And let's see what happens next. That's the excitement of life—what's next."

I've lived that way ever since.

As I keep driving along the 10 in the dark of the early morning, I notice the homes asleep along the side of the freeway. Inside are working class people—laborers, firemen, cops, day workers, people in the services fields—that make our society run. These are people with their names stenciled on their shirts, serving us food, oil, gas, parts, and clothes. People delivering goods and working all night. People who have two or three jobs. People who work hard and get paid just enough to live on the side of a busy freeway.

The first home my father provided for me was a one-bedroom apartment in Flushing, Queens. It was what my father on his cop's salary could afford. Then we moved into a two bedroom the next building over. But at some point, my father saw me and my sisters playing in a concrete area he called "the Snake Pit." He said it looked like a prison holding pen, or the yard where hardened convicts spent their one hour in the sun pumping iron and menacing one another. This, he decided, was not what he wanted for his children.

And so he begged—cajoled—insisted that my mother consider moving out to Long Island. The land of fresh air and potato fields the developers were turning into tract homes. He had a new job by then, working in the flourishing semiconductor industry for Sun Radio. Finally, with great reservations, my mother conceded.

We moved into a split-level house on Wyoming Avenue in North Massapequa, on the South Shore of Long Island. It was 1966. And for the first time in my life, we had a lawn.

The first Saturday we were there, without so much as a stick of proper furniture in the house, my dad and I heard that gardening—*landscaping*—would be the homeowner's responsibility. After a lifetime in Brooklyn and Queens, my dad had no idea what that entailed. But there, encasing our brand-new, middle-class house, was an overgrown expanse of green hair that the neighbors kept calling a lawn, staring up at me and my dad.

We stood in front of the former owner's Toro lawnmower, both of us looking at it like it was a piece of alien technology. We had come from concrete playgrounds; neither of us had ever seen such a sharp-bladed contraption. My dad and I circled it.

"Well, Steven," my dad said finally. "There's some sort of gasoline tank and a pull handle. Let's give it a try."

My dad put one of his legs up on the mower and pulled the cord hard.

Brrrrrr.

He pulled again.

Brrrrrrrrr.

But nothing happened. He looked at the gas tank.

"It's full," he said. "Hmmm."

"Dad? Maybe pull it one more time."

He did, and it started up like a jet engine roaring to life.

"Holy moly!" he yelled to me above the din. "What do we do now, son? Push it?"

He stood behind this new monstrosity, spitting out grass from its undercarriage and raring to get to its purpose. I stood next to my dad—a pair of city rubes in shorts, my skinny legs next to his muscular ones—and we began to push. We could see the cut grass behind us.

"It's working!" he said. "We are cutting grass!"

I watched as a neatly trimmed emerald path appeared behind the mower and looked with awe up at my father. He was a farmer! Paul Bunyan of the Lawn! And we had a house of our very own. As we mowed the lawn together for the first time, my mother and my two sisters came out to watch us, all three wearing cleaning rags on their heads.

"Stanley, you're mowing the grass! How exciting! Look, girls!"

"It's called a lawn, Ann. And Steven is helping. Look at your boy, seven years old and mowing a lawn like a proper suburbanite!"

"I'm a suburbanite?" I said, turning the unfamiliar word over in my mouth. "What's that?"

"It means we live in a house!" my mother yelled above the symphony of the mower blades. "With our very own lawn!"

I watched my father push that Toro until there was nothing left but a carpet of freshly cut delight. His legs were so strong.

They were still on Wyoming Avenue in the summer of 2016 when my sister Susan came by to tell them she had news.

My parents' house was a warm-weather retreat. I planted a thousand impatiens; they surrounded the house like so many candy niblets. The pool was bluer than it should be, and my dad was sitting on the patio with a silver reflector, drinking in that vitamin D. In my mind, Frankie Valli was playing, the air humid like it was giving us all a hug. A Long Island dream.

My parents had sold the original house on Wyoming Avenue to Susan and Bob when they moved down to Florida to take care of my grandmother Kate and her sister Rose. A few years later, they moved back up north to be with the grandkids. The house smack dab across the street from where we grew up came up for sale. They bought it and lived there for fifteen years.

We had a great thing going on Wyoming Avenue. I'd gotten an apartment on the Upper West Side when my mother was diagnosed with breast cancer so that I could see them every day. I'd come out early in the morning and do some chores while they slept: laundry, dishes, planting impatiens in the summer and bulbs in October. I got to see my sister, my parents, and my best friend, Joe. We'd all sit around the kitchen table and talk. What a gift it was to have that kind of closeness. To listen to my father's stories, full of drama and Guttenberg family lore, and my mother's family stories, funny and shocking and meaningful. That glass table was a place I could refuel. And laugh.

Sue came into the backyard of my parents' house—one side of her face happy, the other not so much.

"Bob got an offer he can't refuse, so we're heading to Scottsdale."

She waited. My father put his silver tanner down.

"Arizona?"

"Yes. And we want you and Mom to come with us."

Scraaaaatch. The record stopped.

My parents decided they would go. It was an adjustment for all of us. I'd built a life in New York; my career and personal life grew in muscular fashion. But now, Arizona.

I remember watching my father as he sat in the backyard of the house in Arizona, staring at the cinderblock wall the night before the first dialysis session. I'd driven in that day to be with him at the house Susan and Bob built in the development out there. These are the new neighborhoods: gated, walled, and separated from the active world. There's something safe amid the man-made gathering spots, the streets planned and designed. But they aren't where we came from, where communities sprang from necessity. A shoe store grew from a mom and pop deciding to sell some leather. Homes were built by individual families. Somehow it worked out. Here, my parents are in a gated world, where everything is a car drive away. No candy store on the corner; no neighbors they know; no old friend down the block.

Dad's coal black eyes stared at the wall, beige like everything else in Arizona. Beige was the life of going to Target—the excitement of the day. I watched him from the window as he stared at the wall, waiting for the dialysis to start. I watched this guy who always had something to do at work, around the house, or for us kids. And now he was waiting for his blood to be cleaned. For his new life. And ours. Each of us, in our own way, was trying to deal with the train that we could see way down the tracks. Some of us dreading it, some of us trying to welcome it.

But going to a dialysis clinic three times a week is not what anyone would want.

The backyard in Massapequa was my classroom. I would sit and listen to Dad's stories of Brooklyn, of a time without technology. It was a time when one had more control.

Dad visited me on sets often. He loved the action, the fascinating people, and the crafts service table. I loved having him at work. Everyone loved him.

Chapter THREE

No sleep that night before the first dialysis session. Morning came, and we packed what we thought Dad would need for the session, even though we had no real idea: a few pillows, some water, a magazine, and some candy. Like we were going to sit and wait while Dad was at the dentist. It was noticeably quiet. My mother was trying for whatever positivity she could muster. There were slow movements from all of us—me, my mom, Emily, and Susan. The lethargy of walking into something we knew was going to be existence-changing. But how?

The car crammed with our bodies slid into the parking lot. It didn't look like the sort of place a medical facility belonged. Next door was a dog groomer, a tax preparer, a pool cleaning service, and not one but two hair salons. And, nestled within all that: a Fresenius Dialysis Center.

"Park in the handicap spot," my father said. "We've got a sticker."

My father, still in charge, as he slowly swung his legs out from the shotgun seat. He looked up at the sign for the center, shook his head, and looked at me.

"I can't believe this."

The lobby was weathered linoleum, the pre-cut floor mottled with stains. The walls were pea green with some handmade artwork posted around illustrating information on fluids, phosphates, and potassium.

The cartoon drawings against the green palate gave the room a hospital feel. A few other lost souls sat in the waiting room. A man in his work outfit, the name "Sherman" embroidered on his overalls, sat touching the large fistula on his arm. A woman in a wheelchair sat with her head down, but her eyes searched us for something. I said hello. Later, I would learn her name is Barbara.

"Could you move me closer to the TV?" she said. "I can't hear."

I pushed Barbara towards *Let's Make a Deal*.

"Thank you," she said. "I used to be able to walk."

She was so thin. I noticed my own breathing, shallow and anxious. When I looked over at my father, he rolled his eyes at me. I think there's this desire, or an initial impulse at least, to want to distance ourselves from those who are more infirm than us. But eventually compassion oozes from us, if you've got a heart. And we were going to need a lot of heart for this journey.

The receptionist behind the sliding glass booth looked through the documents my sister had prepared.

"Stanley, huh?" she said. "Is this the right day? I don't see him on the list."

"Good, let's go," my father said, half-kidding. Half.

"Oh, here he is," she said. "They had him marked on a different day. Hi, Stanley. Do you like Stan or Stanley?"

My father, on top of everything else, had hearing problems. Not only from age, but also from a shell that exploded near him in Korea. It made his ears ring, and he had trouble sometimes making out words.

"What did she say?" my father said, looking to my sister.

Barbara, the tiny bird-like lady in the wheelchair, woke up.

"She wants to know what you like to be called," she said.

Dad sat up. He had purpose now, and the blood came back to his face. Blood, waiting to be detoxified.

"Stanley, he likes Stanley," my mother answered politely.

"What? What do they want to know?" my father said, looking at the ceiling and asking G-d for help.

"What you like to be called."

"I don't care. Stanley, Stanley."

I watched my dad as he waited. But when his eyes caught mine, I looked away. I wanted him to think I wasn't worried, so that he wouldn't worry. I didn't know if I was fooling either of us. A few more people came shuffling in, glum and listless. My father kept looking at me, shrugging and shaking his head.

A nurse came out through the door to the treatment room and said hello to Barbara. Barbara looked over at my father.

"His name is Stanley," she said.

"My first question answered," the nurse said. "Stanley, would you like to come with me?"

It's pitch black now on the road as I keep making my way along the 10. I see a set of cherry lights on the shoulder; a young policeman has his flashlight on the interior of a car.

I got my first ticket on this drive a year ago. I'd been making the trip for a few months, taking the speed limit for granted. I hadn't seen a cop for miles, so I pushed the speed to ninety. It felt like a safe enough gallop—not like I was going a hundred—and anyway who would know, with me out there alone and no one nearby? Except for those two red lights in my rearview mirror. How did they come so fast? Does everything bad come out of nowhere?

I pulled over to the right shoulder and put my hands on the wheel, ten and two. Two officers approached me on either side. I saw a flashlight coming from the left and heard a voice coming from the right. Scared the daylights out of me.

"You were going pretty fast there, partner," the officer on my right said. He was smiling.

"Pulling ninety-four, big guy," said the cop on my left. Way too close to me. "License and registration, please."

I asked if I could go to my glove compartment for my registration. The cop told me to make sure I moved real slow. I got the document, but when I reached back for my wallet in my back pocket, I could feel them both bristle.

"Whoa, what are you trying to do?" said the one on the right, backing away from the car, the bright glare of their flashlights still trained on me.

"Get my license?" I said, trying to sound as innocent as possible.

"Tell us the next time you want to move your hands."

I could feel the guy on the left breathing harder now, like he was excited.

I gave them my license and one of them went back to their cruiser. He came back about ten minutes later and told me they had to cite me.

"Drive more carefully out here," he said. "We're watching you, buddy."

I pulled out slowly onto the empty highway and saw their lights recede behind me. That was not pleasant. Ticket number one.

As I slow down to crane my neck, the young cop turns towards me, his cap off, and his hair and skin dark like my father's. He watches me drive slowly by, and our eyes meet. I look ahead and press my right foot on the pedal. He sure looked like my young father.

It's 1963. Spring. Still some remnants of the cold in New York, but everything was starting to feel new and hopeful. The shrubs all looked like they had crewcuts; some were even starting to get full leaves on them. Crocuses and daffodils came up early this year, and everyone kept their windows open. The air was sweet.

My dad put on his new uniform, fresh from the cleaners. He had joined the NYPD at the advice of a friend, who worked Vice in the "Gold Arm" Precinct. They called it that because there were more payoffs in those ten square blocks than in all the rest of New York State. And this friend—who will go unnamed here—was in the middle of it. He was a bag man who collected the monies that certain nefarious men bestowed upon the NYPD. But my dad did everything by the book, which meant there was no money for walking the beat six days a week beyond the forty-eight dollars a week. Forty-eight dollars to support a wife and two kids. The rent alone was seventy-five dollars a month. But he was clean—he wanted nothing to do with payoffs. It didn't make him popular. But it made him his own man.

My father took his gun from the lockbox and examined himself in the mirror. New York's finest and handsome as all get out. My mother loved him in that uniform. She worried about him too, but she knew how much he loved it, and she supported him.

He was a beat cop, out on the street. Helping people, protecting them, and using his physical prowess to keep the Seventeenth Precinct and its people safe. There were no walkie-talkies yet, just call boxes on the corners—a hotline from the streets back to the precinct. So, if something happened—like, say, a maniac with an axe coming down Forty-Third and Eighth—the only way to let the station know was to hop into a lonely box on the corner.

Which was what happened.

My father was on his own that day—his old, grizzled partner off somewhere else—and a small old lady ran up to him, screaming something in Spanish. She was trying to make herself understood to the young police officer, and my father watched her pick her hands up together and pantomime smashing something beneath her. She pointed behind her, and there he was: a six-foot-eight, leather-clad psycho, swinging an axe.

The axe was massive—giant—whipping to-and-fro. And coming straight for my father, intent, apparently, on cutting him in half. He was fast too, cursing as he came at him. So, my father pulled his weapon, but he didn't want to fire—the man was obviously out of his mind.

But if he wasn't going to shoot, what could he do? Like any good cop, he ran, yelling for the maniac to follow him, trying to keep him away from the growing crowd of onlookers. He made it to the call box with the axe-wielding man still half a block behind him.

"Hello, Seventeenth Precinct."

"This is Officer Stanley…gotta run!"

The maniac missed him by a few inches. My father took his gun out again. Backing up, he tried to reason with the man.

"Come on," he pleaded. "I've got a gun; you've got an axe. Who do you think will win?"

The maniac hoisted the axe up over his head and set his sights on Dad.

"Me!" he shouted.

Swack!

The axe missed my dad and hit the concrete. My father ran again and made it to the next call box. But he was getting tired.

"Hello, Seventeenth Precinct."

"Yeah, gotta talk quick, Stanley Guttenberg, there's a crazy man here on Forty-Third with an axe and I need—gotta run!"

This went on for blocks: the axe man chasing my father from call box to call box until finally he got through to the station that he needed backup. About twenty big cops showed up and surrounded the man.

"Take it easy with this guy," he said. "He's not in his right mind."

The other cops rushed the man, forty arms throwing him to the ground. My father could only watch as they beat the hell out of him.

Heading home that night on the subway, at the stop before Main Street, my father held the door open for a woman trying to squeeze onto the train. She squeezed through and fell right into him, still holding the custard birthday cake she was carrying. His uniform, so fresh and clean at the beginning of the day, was now covered in vanilla icing. On top of almost getting cut in half, he got caked.

He walked into our apartment, sweaty and covered in cake. And my mother laughed—oh how she laughed. They had a lot of fun in those days.

"You're my hero," she said, putting me on the kitchen counter to try and wipe the cake off. My dad picked me up in his arms and, with his finger, fed me some of that deliriously happy vanilla cake before my mom sent him down to clean off with the hose behind the apartment building. He gave my mom a kiss on the way out the door, and we listened to him bang down the stairway, two steps at a time.

"Your dad is the greatest," she whispered to me. I already knew.

"Hi, Dad. Are you up?"

I was back out in Hollywood, still trying to make it big as an actor. My dad called every day to check in on me and talk about how it was going. Our deal was that I waited for him to call me so he could use his office phone for the long-distance call. But that day I was too excited to wait.

"What the... Steven, you're calling me?"

"I have an audition for a movie today—no, a screen test—and I'm wearing your Police Academy shirt."

"My old shirt from the NYPD Academy? Why?"

"Dad, it's a movie about the Police Academy!"

"The New York Academy?"

"That's the one. Warner Brothers is casting for the lead, and I thought your shirt would bring me luck."

"Well, it was good for me, son. I got in on the first week's exams and physical endurance tests. I hope it's clean."

My dad got a laugh out of that one.

"I'll tell you after. I gotta go—it's at nine a.m."

I drove up to the Warner Brothers gates on Olive Avenue. At every audition I'd had there before, I'd had to park on the street. But maybe this time, I thought, they'd let me in. I asked the guard, and he shook his head no, thoroughly unimpressed to hear about my screen test for some unknown movie.

I drove for what seemed like hours up and down the side streets, trying to squeeze my tiny Toyota Corolla into a parking space. An older man came out of his house, and I noticed him watching me as I tried to wedge my car into space after space, none of them big enough for me.

"Hey, kid!" he called out. "You need to park for an audition?"

"Yeah, but I can't find anything."

A look came over his face, something like empathy.

"I'm an actor," he said. "I know what it's like. You can park in my driveway."

"Really?" I was suspicious—it's part of being from New York—but I was also running out of options. "And you won't have me towed or anything?"

"I've spent my whole life looking for parking in LA. You can park on my lawn." He gestured to the grass at the front of his house, covered with the tread marks of other tires. "You aren't the only one."

I put my car in front of his big bay windows and locked it. I turned to go.

"Kid," he said. "You have to give me the keys."

Here, I thought, was the catch.

"What the…you're gonna steal my car!"

"You'll just have to trust me. You're going to have to start trusting strangers, kid, if you're going to stay an actor."

He looked at me, and I stared right back, neither of us breaking eye contact.

"Okay," I said finally, handing him the keys to my precious Toyota. "It's against my better judgement, but okay."

"It'll be here when you get back. Promise."

I ran from his house to the lot, wondering the whole time what he was going to do with the car. Steal it? Send it to Mexico to be stripped for parts? It was three long blocks before, finally, I got to the gate and tried to put any thought of my car out of my mind. The guard waved me through, and I searched for Stage Eleven, the one with the red flashing light that says "do not enter." I waited until the spinning red globe slowed to a stop and then pulled the thousand-pound door open.

Someone had been testing before me. I heard laughter, and then applause. An assistant director approached me.

"You're sweating like no one else. You okay?"

I told him that I ran all the way there because I wasn't allowed to park on the lot. He nodded.

"Yeah, we couldn't give out two spots—David, the other guy testing, got it. Sorry. Here's a rag, wipe your face, man."

David came off the set like he was on vacation, heading back from the pool for a piña colada in the lobby.

"You look like you came through a carwash!" he said with a big smile. "The director and crew are so great—you're gonna love it. Break a leg, man." Cool as a cucumber.

The director was a good-natured man from the South, with a big grin and an inviting Atlanta accent.

"Guttenberg, you okay? Need time to get yourself together?" he said. "Tell you the truth, you got a hell of a lot of competition. David was great. He can sing and dance too...."

And then he noticed what I was wearing.

"Is that a real Police Academy shirt?"

"Yeah, my father was a cop."

"Well, get on up there, Steve, and let's see what you can do."

I walked onto the set. The lights were hot as the sun, and the crew was hungry, tired, and bored. I even saw a guy knitting. Knitting! They rolled the camera, and I started to do the scene with a casting associate who was just as hungry, tired, and bored as everyone else. I thought I had some game, but it quickly became clear that I didn't. There were no laughs. No applause.

I walked off the set, and the director was emotionless.

"Good job," he said vaguely. "Thanks for coming in."

I walked out of the soundstage, past the guard with my head hung low. I crawled back to the house. My car was still there, the man sitting out on the lawn in a lounge chair.

"You didn't get it?" he said. He flipped me the keys.

"No way. It was quiet as a mouse on the set."

"You never know, kid. If you get it…"

"I won't."

"If you get it, you owe me a beer. No domestic junk either. Foreign suds."

I drove home, staring out at the cold and unloving 101 freeway. I pulled up to my apartment and called my agent.

"I was just going to call you," he said.

"I feel terrible," I said. "They loved that guy David. They clapped for him. They laughed. I feel like crap."

"You got it."

"What?"

"You got it. They developed the test film lickety-split, showed it to the Warner executives, and Jay Cantor stood up and yelled, 'Hire the Jew!' Get to temple and thank your rabbi."

I did one better than that. I drove all the way back to the Good Samaritan's house and parked in my spot on his lawn. His door opened up.

"That was fast," he said. "Want a shoulder to cry on?"

I opened my trunk and pulled out a case of Heineken.

"Want a beer?"

We went to Musso and Frank, an old Hollywood standard, as it reminded Dad of New York. Great waiters. Like Peter Luger in New York.

My dad was a fitness buff, a gym rat who gave me the
gift of self-care, of exercise and moderation of diet. He
could do handstands for hours and lift weights heavier
than a man of his size should have been able to. He was a
specimen.

Chapter FOUR

The car is a mess. There are muffin crumbs under my feet, coffee stains on my seat, and sticky goo on the center console. I don't clean it; things don't mean that much to me. I've never been a car guy. I use them to get here and there. The only car I ever took good care of was the Chrysler New Yorker my dad gave me as a senior in high school. It was his company car, and I saw how much it meant to him, the way he cared for it, and I felt an obligation to keep it pristine.

I did have a Ferrari, and then a Mercedes. But since then, I've been the guy with the modest car, the object of ridicule among my car-loving, testosterone-fueled friends. Every car of mine has been driven to its limits, at least a hundred thousand miles. If a door gets crunched in a misjudged rub against a parking lot wall, it gets replaced by the cheapest thing I can find. The body shop knows by now that I'm no fancy customer; anything that fits works for me. How many times have I heard, "Gute, this car looks like crap—give it to the dump and buy something new"? But I never do.

The lights on the car lots start to dim in the early morning dark. Are they on automatic timers? Home Depot opens at seven. In-N-Out Burger opens at ten. These are the things I know now without ever really thinking about them, having learned them drive after drive with nothing to do but think and watch the road. I check my gas gauge—still almost full.

I push the driver's side window all the way down. I want to feel the air on my face, to wake me up a little. I can feel the wind cleaning the car of its rank smell. Maybe my thoughts too, if I'm lucky. I can feel my breathing starting to get deeper—my lungs picking up that there's some fresh oxygen wafting through. Still dark outside.

That first day at dialysis, as the nurse led us into the room, I was having a little trouble breathing. It was so cold in that room—an artificial cold that kept forcing itself down my throat before my lungs spit it automatically back out. Like a knife pulling through my chest. I could feel the goosebumps on my arms—was that from the cold too, or just nerves? Usually when I'm nervous, I sweat like crazy. No sweating in this cold, though.

The room was massive—twenty-four chairs for the patients, each looking like a first-class seat on a Boeing. But we all knew this was no pleasure trip. Next to each chair was a machine, four feet tall, with a digital screen that took true study to figure out. Beneath the digital readout was a circular pinwheel, with two rubber tubes leading in opposite directions. And to the right was the actual dialyzer, which brings the blood—cooled to thirty-four degrees—through its spongelike interior, light beige before it receives the precious fluid.

The five of us stood in the middle of the room, our feet frozen. The people hooked up to the machines were in a variety of physical states. There were seniors with their eyes closed, gray hair falling over their faces; there were weary-looking men and women with ailments that couldn't be deciphered from a cursory glance; heavy people, thin-as-rails people, young people. The youngsters were the ones who caught my eye. To think they had only just started on life's journey and were now hooked up to these machines for life. One of the young girls had a portal in her chest. Her family sat by her side for a few minutes and then got up to go. She was blind and held her hand to her portal, earphones tugging her head.

"Hey, family," said a kind-eyed Black man with a head of curly hair. "It's going to be okay. Just a bit of a shock, isn't it? Your first day?"

The man had such a friendly face, and a wide smile revealing yellowed teeth.

"Yeah, my dad's."

"Gotcha. I'll be seeing a lot of you then. I'm Dave."

His chest portal had blood weaving its way through the rubber tube into the machine and another tube returning it to his chest: arterial and venous. He smiled through a beard, a little straggly but still regal. Bags of half-eaten food sat next to him.

"My kids bring me McDonald's for lunch. Your dad's going to want to eat—it's a three- or four-hour pull here." He grabbed my hand. "Don't be scared. It's going to be alright—promise."

He had kind eyes. People there were extra sensitive—they could feel me shaking inside. I stood, watching the blood meander through the two tubes in his chest, like a lazy sippy cup straw attached to a toddler's lips. Dave saw me put my hands in my pockets against the artificial cold and smiled at me. His eyes, slightly yellow like his teeth, were full of love for me.

"Cold in here, huh? You'll get used to it. Keeps the bugs at bay. Cold is good. The colder the better."

But despite what Dave said, I was having trouble with it. It felt like there was something wrong with the air—cold shouldn't feel like this.

"You'll all have to put these masks on if you want to stay," Kim, the technician, said. My father watched with his large black eyes as we each fitted the masks over our faces.

Kim had bright candy-red hair and a smock with her name colorfully stenciled across the chest. I wondered—did the cold affect her too? She gestured towards the chair.

"Mr. Guttenberg, want to take a seat here?"

I could see my dad didn't want to sit down. He didn't want to be there at all. He wanted to go home. We all did. Finally, he took a deep breath, looked at us, and shrugged. A shrug that meant not "who cares?" but instead "what can I do?" I saw more shrugs from him that day than I had ever seen before. He squished back into the seat.

"Family, you can grab some chairs if you like," Kim said. I went to grab a couple of metal folding chairs.

"I'll stand," my mother said, ramrod straight.

The room was full of noise from the machines—twenty-four of them, all beeping out of sync. Kim put a blood pressure sleeve on my dad.

"Do you have to do that?" my mother asked.

"Yes, Mrs. Guttenberg," she said. "It's important to monitor his blood pressure while he's on the machine. You'll get used to it."

"Stanley, is it too tight?"

"It's okay. I'm okay."

My father was looking at the man across the way, slumped into his seat, sadly staring out vacantly into space.

"That's not you, Dad," I whispered. I took one of his hands in mine, and he squeezed. "That man has something different than you."

He sighed again.

"I know, I know."

Kim started to prepare a few needles with different thickness.

"We have to see what circumference your father's fistula can maintain. We'll start small today, sixteen millimeters, and go from there."

My mother watched like a hawk guarding her eggs as Kim tapped the enormous vein protruding from my father's arm.

"Nice thrill," she said, finding a spot. She inserted a needle, and my father winced.

"Stanley," my mother said, moving forward a step. "Does that hurt?"

"It's okay. I felt it a little."

The blood started to squeeze its way through the tube.

"Ready for the next one?" Kim asked. "That was the outie—the arterial. Now the innie—the venous."

"Wait," my mother said before Kim could insert the next needle. She took my father's arm. "Wait. Just, let him rest a second."

My father put his hand on top of my mother's. She stared into his eyes. I could hear them breathing together that cold, cold air.

"Let him rest," my mother said. Then she sat down.

After a minute, Kim went back to preparing the needle. My father started to take off the blood pressure cuff.

Time *to* Thank

"You'll need to keep that on, Stanley," she said. Kim pushed in the second needle—a big, thick metal cylinder. It went deep; it needed to.

"I didn't really feel that one," he said.

Kim smiled.

"Good. That's my aim, for you not to feel it."

"Aim," my father said, smiling back. "I get it."

She reclined my father's seat; his feet went up, his eyes closed, and his head tilted back like his flight had finally reached cruising altitude. But no dinner service on this flight, just two tubes with thirty-four-degree blood coursing through. Kim keyed in what felt like a thousand different keyboard strokes onto the digital screen. The machine's circular wheel began to spin. My father opened his eyes, and we all leaned in to watch. Blood started to feed into the machine, and a few seconds later, it returned to my dad through the other tube. Red stripes grew over my father's chest, the beige dialyzer filling up with blood until it turned deep crimson. It started to beat with every pump, as though keeping pace with the heartbeat. It moved—beat, beat—shaking left and right. Like it knew what it was there for, conscious of the hard work of cleaning. My father adjusted his Korean Veteran cap and rested his head back.

"Want to wash the car, Steven?"

It was summer 1961, and I was three years old. My mom laughed with delight when she heard the suggestion.

"Good, Stanley. Father and son. I like that."

My father loved to wash his cars. He wanted to show his young son how it was done. He was so proud to have a boy—he took me everywhere. His little mascot.

It was a hot summer day on Franklin Avenue in Flushing, Queens. The smell of water on hot concrete has a specific odor that hits your nostrils with a punch. But in the city, with all that brick and asphalt and concrete and metal, it's oddly reassuring. Music was playing throughout the streets: on car radios, out apartment windows, from speakers in front of the local candy store.

It was a perfect day for a detailed cleaning of my parents' Volkswagen bug. My father took me downstairs to wait until a space opened up in front of the apartment building. He put my stroller in the street to save the spot while he ran down the block to move the car. I sat there, sucking my thumb, until he showed up in the bug and moved me into the car. Parallel parked like a pro.

With me in the car, he ran all the way up to our apartment to fill up the bucket in the sink with water and dish soap. He used an undershirt that had seen too many cycles in the washer as his rag. My mother came out of the bedroom with a broom in her hand and saw him at the sink.

"Stanley, why are you sweating like that?"

"I have to get the water to wash the car."

"What the hell is wrong with you? There's a community hose on the side of the building. And where's Steven?"

"He's down in the car."

My mother looked out the window and saw my little blob of a body in the front seat.

"You can't leave a little kid in a car! Get the hell down there!"

He ran down, checked on me, and then got started on washing the car.

It was ninety-four degrees in Queens, humidity at 80 percent. But my father was completely absorbed in his work. He soaped up the bumpers, all the chrome, the hubcaps, and the antenna. Back and forth to the community hose. When he finally stepped back to admire his handiwork, he heard a noise—a groan—and then a yell. And as he went to rinse the windshield, he saw through the glass his little son's face bathed in sweat. He had forgotten me. Maybe that's where I learned to sweat.

"Oh, shit!"

He pulled open the driver's side door, grabbed me, and raised me in the air. I breathed in the hot, humid air, free finally from the heat of the car. And then I started to laugh. He laughed too, holding me high in the air and twirling me in circles. The neighbors were looking at us out their windows, and my mother came out the front door of the building.

"What the hell are you doing?" she said. "Is Steven okay?"

"He just learned how to wash a car! Right, son?"

I was still laughing, as the story goes. Just me and him. Two guys doing a job.

I bought my first house in 1980, when I was twenty-one, and my parents couldn't have been prouder. I think they got more out of it than me, too young to know I was lucky. It was a real adult home, on a street with a hillside behind it. There was a legend that the hill came down years before, the landslide killing a couple who'd lived in the house next door. The man who owned the house before me said that he and his wife would sometimes wake up to find the ghosts standing in their bedroom. But I never saw those phantoms.

It was a cool time for me. My dad got an offer to head a company in Calabasas, and he wanted to try it out for a few months. My mother refused to come out until they gave him a contract. So, the two of us were roomies.

One Saturday, I was out about town and my father was holding down the fort. On Beverly Glen Boulevard, a young and spectacular girl was in the back of a stretch limo. Her name was Carol, but she went by Cindy. She was one of the chosen bunnies that worked in the Playboy Club in Century City, California. I had met her at The Comedy Store on Sunset Boulevard. I can imagine it so clearly: Cindy on the edge of the black and soft Italian leather, as the driver waited to make the turn from Mulholland Drive to Sherview Drive, where my house was.

About a half mile down the road, my father washed the Datsun Z with the T-top in front of my house. He had his shirt off, naked from his belt to the top of his head, save for a pair of aviator Ray-Bans and a US Army Eighty-Second Airborne cap. He was relishing the California sun and the big position he'd garnered at Bonner Electronics.

My dad still loved to wash his cars. There was a set order to the way he worked it: first the hood, then the roof, then the sides, then the rear, and finally, with care, the wheels. Wet, soap, spray.

And as he looked up, that long black hood turned the corner in slow motion. It was sexy, sleek, shiny. My father stood, agog. He looked behind him: Was someone waiting outside their home for this carriage?

The monster stretch Caddy stopped in front of him. Then, just like in the movies, a chauffeur came out. He tipped his cap to my father, whose muscles, wet with the foam, glistened in the golden sun. He often did his handstands in the backyard, the neighbor girls stretching out their windows to see him. He looked like a Greek god, compliments of his regular workouts.

The chauffeur opened the back passenger door, and another movie moment presented itself to the recent arrival to California. One bare leg and then another, both sporting three-inch heels, hit the ground. She had flawless skin, her hair was long, and in her arms sat a box of Belgian chocolate.

"Hi," she said. "Who are you?"

"I'm Stanley."

"Well, Stanley, is Steven home?"

"No, he's not. I'm his father."

"You can't be his father." She looked him up and down. "His father can't be so young."

Gulp.

"Well, ah, I am. Is there anything I can do for you?"

My father was fiercely loyal, but his eyes could see.

"Would you give Steven these chocolates, and tell him I'll see him when he returns?"

"Yes, I will. Who should I say gave them to him?"

"His friend Cindy." She reached toward my father and handed him the gold and white ribboned box. She started to get back in the limousine, but then she turned around.

"Oh, and thanks for your service." She pointed to the green Army cap. Looking him up and down, she said, "I just love a man in uniform…even if it's only a cap and muscles."

The chauffeur dropped his keys, and his mouth dropped open. My father couldn't help himself from saying something to her.

"May I say, you're a beautiful woman."

"You're not too bad yourself, Mr. Guttenberg. Stanley."

The limo and Cindy did a U-turn and drove away toward the horizon, but the story stayed on. It still poured from my dad's lips every so often. He loved it, and the California sun still lit up his olive skin from inside when he told that tale. You should have seen him shirtless. No wonder Cindy teased, "Your dad is a hottie, Steve. Lucky he's a married man."

Maybe another man would have been tempted. But Cindy didn't know Dad.

We traversed California together. Here we are at Patrick's Roadhouse in Pacific Palisades, a home to body builders. My dad fit right in with Arnold Schwarzenegger and Franco Columbu.

The water has forever been a staple in my family's lives. My dad brought us to the Bahamas, and I sucked my stomach in the whole time.

Chapter FIVE

Someone behind me beeps their horn. I look at my speedometer, and it's only reading forty-five miles per hour. It's five a.m. California time, already six in Phoenix.

I text my sister to tell her I'm on the road. My dad is probably awake already; he doesn't sleep well very often and is usually up early. So Susan gets up early too. At this hour, she'll be walking her dog before heading back to the house to make my dad's renal breakfast: a hard-boiled egg, a vegan grilled cheese sandwich, a Boost protein shake, and some decaf coffee. All the liquids are carefully doled out to stay within the thirty-two-ounce daily limit.

I pick up my speed, shaking my head awake and taking a sip from my coffee. I'll stop soon to walk around at an ampm rest stop or something like that. I play with the radio out of a bit of boredom and get the news. An Amtrak train has derailed—it's the lead story, and every station I switch to is running with it. I switch it back off.

I can see a few clouds against the dark sky now. The sunrise keeps peeking over the horizon, but no real sign of her yet. With nothing useful to distract me, I let my thoughts wander even more than usual. Good memories flood my head for once, and I'm so drawn to them. I'm back in 1964, and my dad comes home with a big announcement: tomorrow, we're going to the World's Fair. It makes Disneyland look like some kind of high school project. Here is a vision of the future.

Robot maids! And the rides! My father lifts me and my sister onto each and every ride.

It's true—you really don't know what you have 'til it's gone. I want to linger in those memories, luxuriate in them. I'm definitely not paying attention to the road. I pick up my coffee thermos—

BAM!

The car ahead of me hits the truck ahead of him. I have three seconds to react.

I swerve to the right, hoping no one is coming up behind me, but I check the rearview mirror too late for it to actually make a difference. I get lucky—there's no one to my right, and I fly past the wreck, watching the chaos unfold behind me in the mirror.

I pull over. There's coffee all over the interior of the car and dripping from the rearview mirror. I keep turning my head, sure that somehow the accident will catch up to me. I see the truck getting rear ended, then each car smashing into the one in front of it: a massive pileup. A few cars grind onto the shoulder; one of them hits the guardrail. There's even a little chaos starting up on the other side of the freeway.

I keep driving. I gotta pay attention. I thought I was. These damn memories. I do everything I can to calm down and get off at the next exit. Sure enough, there's the ampm I've been thinking about for miles.

I park and walk in to buy more coffee. On the way back I stop at the car door and, instead of getting back in, I think it might be better for me to go sit on that bench over there for a while. The cold aluminum isn't any sort of welcoming hug, but it's better than getting back in my car. That wreck shook me up.

A van pulls up next to me and a whole extended family empties out—seniors, toddlers, and babies in strollers. A man is left to fill up the tank while everyone else heads into the store. A baby is crying.

"Hey, man," he says, noticing me. "Did you come off the Ten?"

"I did," I say, a little wary. Did I leave the scene of a crime?

"There are cops and ambulances stopping traffic for miles. We just missed it. Did you?"

"Yeah."

"Damn. This fuckin' Ten is dangerous as hell. Now the baby won't stop crying."

"Lucky you and your family are okay."

"Damn straight—we were right behind that fuckin' truck."

I get up—I'm nervous that somehow I'm going to get attached to this accident, and my license is going to get yanked. I've got three tickets already—I'm on thin ice as it is. I make like I'm going back inside the convenience store but instead walk towards the freeway to try and get a look at what's happening.

He's right: traffic on the 10 east appears unending now. This highway is one dicey path to travel. And I've got 350 miles left.

The cab of my car feels cold and empty when I get back inside. I can smell the plastic of the dashboard. My empty Stanley thermos is sideways on the console.

Danger has a way of sneaking up on you when you're on the road. You have to be ready to react when it comes.

It was May 1968. A school night. I was ten years old. I had been asking my father to take me to Adventureland for months—home of the most thrilling rides on Long Island. I had already done my homework.

It was just starting to get warm outside. The humidity hadn't yet reached its summer fullness; this was important because it meant that you could still wear a jacket. My father had a leather jacket, regal and worn down in all the places it was supposed to be. I had the fake leather miniature version. All I wanted to do was walk around Adventureland with my dad and his leather bomber. Like we were a little gang. A gang of Guttenbergs.

I took my jacket out from the downstairs closet. My father was in the garage, dusting off the old Toro, wiping last year's grass off the mower's carriage.

"Dad, I have my leather on. Can we go to Adventureland? Just me and you. Maybe one or two rides? That's it, just one or two? We could be matching."

He had his hands full. I knew this chore was important. I got ready for his "no," ready to turn away.

He sighed and looked at me, putting his hands on the debris he just meticulously collected.

"Steven, I have a lot to do here."

My face fell. He picked up some packing tape.

"But I have to return this to Pergament Hardware. I could do it after Adventureland. You, my little buddy, need to see one or two rides? Then that's what we will do."

Oh, jubilation! I ran upstairs to tell Mom. We got our orders: one or two rides, then back in time for bed.

I sat in the car, comparing our jackets and how they almost matched. It was so cool to be with Dad, just him and me, going to Adventureland. He opened the driver's window and hung his elbow out, and I did the same thing. We were twins. It was everything I could ask for.

I watched my father's smile turn to a frown as he kept watching the rearview mirror.

"This guy is on my tail."

He kept motioning for the car behind to pass him by moving his arm in a circular fashion. I did the same: after all, we were twins, buddies, a leather gang.

"Why won't he—Steven put your arm back in the car."

His voice had changed, more serious than when I was his good-time buddy.

The car swung from behind and went ahead of us but then slowed down, driving a few feet from our bumper.

My father stared at the car and his shoulders went back. "What the…"

So, my father let up on the gas and so did the car. I could see it was a Corvair.

"Doesn't this idiot know that Corvairs blow up if you hit the trunk?"

My father switched lanes; so did the Corvair.

"This is dumb."

He hit the brakes and pulled over to the shoulder. So did the other driver. I started to cry.

"Don't worry, Steven. It's okay."

"Dad, I don't want anything to happen."

"It won't. I'll talk to the man, and we can then go on the rides." He smiled at me and took my chin in his hands. "I know you're afraid, son, but I promise you, nothing will happen."

And he got out of the car.

"No, Dad!"

He walked toward the Corvair. Out of the passenger door came a man dressed in black, twice the size of my father. He was furious, waving his hands back and forth, and approaching my dad.

I could see my dad put up his hands, those soft hands I knew so well. He was asking the guy to calm down, but the giant would have none of that.

He hit my father.

He hit him with so much force that it knocked my dad to the ground. He then walked to my father's side and kicked him. I could tell my father was hurt. And he went to kick him again.

And then, something miraculous happened.

The woman who was driving came out and started to wave her hands to get the man to stop. He turned his head. My father grabbed his leg and pulled him to the ground.

And then, with a single punch, he knocked the man out. Cold.

Dad stood up, said something to the lady, and walked back to the car.

"Steven, could you get me that tape from the back seat?"

I reached back and gave him the bag, feeling for the circle of tape inside.

"And the medicine kit in the glove box—can I have it?"

He walked back to the couple. By then, the woman was on her knees, shaking the man. He wasn't getting up. My dad unspooled the tape, turned the man over, and taped his hands together. He turned him right side up and broke a smelling salt from the medicine kit. The man awoke and sat up like a bull coming to after being shot by a tranquilizer gun. I saw how enormous he was. He struggled while my father gave him a talking to. Then Dad helped him up and deposited him in the Corvair.

Dad got back in the car.

"Steven, stop crying."

I didn't say anything for a few minutes while we drove.

"Why did that man hit you?"

"Just thought I was someone else, son. That's all."

I thought for a moment.

"We have to go home now?"

He looked at me, smiled, and put his hand under my chin as he did before.

"What do you think?"

He drove toward those colored lights of Adventureland.

It was one of the best nights my dad and I ever had. We got home at midnight.

By the time I made it out to Hollywood, of course, my nights got even later.

Back in 1979, I did the most outlandish movie ever. *Can't Stop the Music* was the name, and insanity was the game. The movie starred the Village People, Bruce (now Caitlyn) Jenner, and Valerie Perrine. The director was Nancy Walker, a talented actress who'd never had her hands around a viewfinder until now. It was the most expensive movie made that year, and the money flowed endlessly: not just on the set, but also in the crazy parties that the production team threw.

It was the morning after one of these parties—and these were at least once a week—that my dad woke me up with one of his daily six a.m. phone calls. I put him on speakerphone as I groggily got out of bed and started washing up, telling him about the party the whole time.

"I was at the producer Allan Carr's house for a crazy party. James Caan used to own the house. Dad, there's a basketball hoop in the living room!"

"Now that's different."

My dad was always cool as a cucumber when I told him about all the "different" things I saw in Hollywood.

"The party—what was it like? And I hope you put on cologne. It's the sign of a cultured man, and that's what you are, Steven."

This had been my father's belief ever since his old boss at Sun Radio taught him about different fragrances. According to legend, Sam's scents were so beguiling that he could walk into a sale and make a buyer take every cathode ray tube he had on him, and then some. So, my father, wanting to emulate Sam, began experimenting with every exotic fragrance ever known to man. There was Hai Karate, Brut, Old Spice, Aqua Velva, English Leather, Pinaud for everyday use, and then the special stuff: Faberge Babe, Prince Matchabelli, and Jovan Musk for Men. I could still remember getting ready in the bathroom on Wyoming Avenue, hoping that it was going to be the day that my dad looked over from his sink and said, "Today, and I mean today, is a Prince Matchabelli day. You want a sprinkle?" There was nothing better than when my dad shared a little of his cologne.

"I wore Brut, Dad," I told him as I splashed some cold water on my face and kept talking about the party.

The first thing I noticed as I walked up the long driveway to the house were all the men in bathing suits. Every ten feet or so stood a muscular man in a bathing suit, each bigger and beefier than the man before him. And each one held a different alcohol: the first had tequila, the second vodka, and the third gin. All of them stared straight ahead like a Beefeater in front of Buckingham Palace.

The house was a massive Tudor and looked more like a private school than a private home. I walked through the triple doors—not double, but triple!—and was greeted by a lady wearing only a painted tuxedo on her body, offering up a bowl of capsules like they were complimentary mints. I laughed and shook my head, taking in the crowd as I made my way across the room. The people were dressed like nothing I had ever seen before: feathers and boas, silver-spangled suits, sunglasses at night. I headed over to the food, where every dish imaginable seemed to be arrayed before me, all attended by ten tanned and svelte ladies wearing only bikinis. The music, naturally, was pure funky disco.

I wandered around until I found the host: Allan Carr, producer extraordinaire. He was standing in the center of some of the most beautiful people I'd ever seen. He noticed me and waved me over.

"Steven, come meet the most exciting people on the planet."

I said hello to each and every one of them. But as they talked, I started looking around. And I noticed a line of people heading towards the steps that led down to a basement.

I excused myself and followed the crowd down the silver stairs, listening as a sound grew louder all around me. Once I reached the bottom, I saw what everyone was coming down for: I was in the middle of a full-fledged, multi-platinum, pulse-pounding, lights-poppin' disco, with what had to be easily a hundred bodies movin' to the groovin'. Allan had his own nightclub in his house!

The dance floor seemed to go on for miles, and I slipped through sweaty bodies, each more gorgeous than the next. I felt an arm grab me around the waist and turned to see a woman I recognized from some detective show, though I couldn't remember her name. We danced until the wee hours, but as suddenly as she appeared, she vanished without a word.

At the end of the night, I walked back up the stairs, grabbed myself a goody bag filled with swag from the movie, and stuffed as much food into it as I could from the buffet—I've always been thrifty, but even more so back in my salad days, and this would feed me for a week. I walked down the driveway, stepping over bodies sleeping, resting, and grinding on each other, got into my Corolla, and drove back to my studio apartment in Westwood. My Huckapoo shirt and tight nylon pants were completely soaked through with sweat.

"It was a grand old time, Dad. Hollywood style."

"That's dangerous territory, Steven. Make sure you always know what's going on around you. People get crazy with parties like that."

"Like I said, that was one crazy, crazy party."

"I get it, I get it. Now go start your day! Get back in that car and beat the bushes around Hollywood! I love you."

That's just what I did. I was armed with my father's love, which gave me the energy and confidence to swim with the Hollywood sharks in pursuit of my dream.

"Stanley, you want a pillow?" my mother said, producing a small fluff from her bag. She put it behind my father's head and kissed him before sitting back down, shaking her head and looking at the ground.

The first day at dialysis felt as though it would never end. Once he was settled in, I began to listen to the sounds of the room—all those clicks and beeps. Each machine working with all its might. Technicians moving back and forth between patients, making sure everything was working as it should. Some people were with their families, others with caretakers sitting behind them in starched, white uniforms. The individual monitors all blared different shows—reality TV, CNN, sports.

After a time, Dave called me over.

"If you go out, bring me a coffee if you can. I'm a bit busy," he said, pointing to the pair of red tubes on his side. The portal in his chest rose with every breath. He picked up his Big Mac and took a bite, giggling as he chewed. The dialyzer rose and fell in concert with his beating heart. "I'm an ordained minister too, if you ever need."

"Hey, asshole, I'm going to be sick."

A thin man huddled under a blanket across the room started to heave. Violently. Every tech and RN rushed over to him. In unison, they donned plastic smocks, face shields, and gloves. All the machines were still blaring their beeps and alarms. His wife was yelling for help. The head RN sat close to the man, directing the others.

"Everybody back up!"

Within moments, there was a plastic wall around him, prepared for what was coming. Then—*blurp*—the man projectile vomited for thirty seconds. And I mean, it looked like a gallon of his insides. The plastic caught most of the yellow glurp, with only a few of the techs getting splattered. They pushed their face shields down as one, like Trojan warriors.

As soon as it had started, it was over. The plastic came down, face shields and aprons taken off, and the man leaned back against his chair in relief. The staff returned to their normal duties. Just like that.

We were frozen, the four of us wide-eyed, staring at the scene. My father wasn't blinking. The man finished cleaning himself up and opened a magazine. His wife changed the channel of their television. Like nothing happened.

"Happens often around here," Kim said, adjusting a few buttons on our digital screen. "Especially the people with diabetes. It's not pretty, but it happens."

It took us all night to get over that. What shook me was how private it felt, like something I wasn't supposed to see.

"You're doing great, Stanley," Kim said. "You're way ahead of the game."

I began to look at the people around us. A woman handed a thin man with old clothes a cup from Starbucks. I noticed that he was missing a leg. A tall, lanky man with the look of an ex-athlete sat with tubes in his portal as his wife knitted something; together, they watched Fox. A man was sleeping with his head back, his mouth agape. His caretaker was eating her lunch, her blue uniform bunched up.

Then there was Brad. He was a young man in his thirties, wearing pajamas, and I couldn't help but notice him when he came into the center. He was full of energy, carrying a bag of goodies that he unloaded once he got to his seat. Candy, moisturizer, magazines, his telephone, and his iPad. Once he was settled, he actually started to prepare his own fistula.

"Brad can stick himself," Kim said to me as she changed her gloves. "We just watch and make sure he's not going to bleed. And he hooks himself up for four hours a day. Three days a week, every week. He's been doing this for ten years; he's an old pro."

He was like the Elvis of the clinic: young and energetic. As I watched him, I thought about what his life must be like. Was he like other, vital thirty-year-olds outside this little dialysis world? The hustlers, the young men with no limits, confident and vibrant? I watched as Brad put a tourniquet around his bicep. He pulled the eighteen-millimeter needle towards his fistula and stuck himself. This guy, I thought, is one tough mother. Alarms going off; machines buzzing; techs and RNs running around. Meanwhile, Brad hooked himself up like a trucker gassing his Mack on the highway.

He looked over at me with a half-smile, like he knew something I didn't. He kept staring as he adjusted his tubes.

I tried hard to be as nice to everyone working there as I could. I wanted them all on our side—to give my father a little more attention, watch his numbers a little more closely. Would any of that make this easier for him? I wanted to find a way to turn this heavy load into cotton candy.

The hours moved ahead, slow and sluggish. My father looked up at me again, his light eyebrows arched. It was like he was shrugging with his eyes, saying, "What can I do? I'm here." I nodded in reply. I wanted to touch him, to comfort him, as he watched his blood go in and out. But each time he shook me off.

"I'm alright," he said.

Finally, the dialysis machine issued a loud alarm. We were done. The green light on the top of the machine switched over to red. Kim came over and asked my father how he was feeling.

"Okay," he said, shaking his head.

"Okay is okay," Kim said. "I'm going to take both the needles out. I'm good at it. You didn't feel them going in today too much?"

"I did," my father said with a smile. He has a charming honesty. He was so genuine, so different from my show business world. Kim got ready to extract the needles.

"One of you can learn how to hold the injection sites," she said.

My sister Susan stood up.

"I'll do it."

I still thought of Susan as a kid sometimes—the little sister I used to make milkshakes for, hiding a gum ball at the bottom of her kiddie sugar delight. But she's fifty now, not a curly-haired little kid sucking on her thumb or the runner-up prom queen. She is a wife, a mother, a former publishing executive with a master's in education. She put on the gloves, and Kim pointed to two bandages.

"Just hold here," she said.

Susan held tight for ten minutes. She sighed when the time was done, and Kim bandaged my father's fistula. The RN came by—she wanted to listen to his heart and lungs. I started to think about how good the Arizona heat was going to feel after so many hours in the cold.

My father was strong enough to walk out of the center on his own and straight to the car. We talked for a little while on the drive, but after a time we lapsed into silence. All of us took a deep breath when we pulled into the driveway.

See you in two days.

My dad was a He-Man, but he let me kiss him all the time. Military men are quite stoic, but Dad let loose with his affection.

I was accepted for membership in the Academy of
Motion Picture Arts and Sciences, and my folks insisted
we go to the Academy on July 4th. It was closed, but
the security guard let us in.

Chapter SIX

I get back on the road and drive in silence for a time. I keep watching the clock, thinking about when to call Arizona. I wait until the clock ticks over to five thirty.

"Steven, is that you?"

My dad's voice is thin and scratchy—it's early in the day, but still, the timbre jars me. In my head, I'm still hearing his voice from fifty years ago: full, rich, and smooth. At least his accent is still the same, and it's comforting to hear his voice.

"Where are you?" he says. "Did you hit Palm Springs yet?"

He loves to know coordinates. I think about telling him about the crash but shake off the idea.

"I'm somewhere on the Ten freeway. Not sure where."

"Did you know those were the coordinates for my first mission in Korea? The code name was Tenten."

"Really?"

"Yes, really! And don't get any tickets, you damn speeder."

"I got a ticket so I could come see you."

"Yeah, yeah, I know all about it. Roger that. Later."

He hands the phone over to my sister Sue.

"He's a ball of energy," she says. "The fistula was bleeding, but I got it under control. And Steven? No tickets."

Click.

I got my second speeding ticket a few months after the first. Rain was misting the road, and I was cruising along. I like to go fast when it's four in the morning and there are no other cars on the road. That's the danger of a smooth ride: the cab shakes the same whether I'm going thirty-five or ninety-five.

I had the news blaring in my ears, wearing the new AirPods Emily bought me. Lester Holt was telling me about last night's news, and I was thinking that multitasking suited me. I could learn about current events, eat my oatmeal, and drink my coffee, all while pointing my car towards Arizona.

I switched over from Lester to Metallica, thinking I needed a little more *oomph* to wake me up. I picked up speed; nothing could stop me now.

Except…

A cop car appeared from my right side, driving parallel to me with his red lights on. My first thought was, does he need to pass me for some reason? I raised my hand in a friendly "hello" and slowed down. He must have caught someone, I thought. Then I looked at my speedometer: ninety-five. No way!

I looked over at the cop again, and he screamed into the megaphone on top of his car.

"Pull over!"

I did just that. Metallica faded to nothing as I took the ear buds out and sat waiting for the storm.

"What the hell?" the cop asked. "You were going ninety-five, man. And wearing headphones? Were you really driving with those things in your ears?"

I could only stutter—I had nothing else to say.

"License and registration. G-d, I was following you for ten miles, siren on full blast, and you still didn't hear me!"

More stuttering from me.

"Wait here," he said, stalking back to his cruiser.

This was not good.

He came back after ten minutes, shaking his head.

"I gave you a break and only clocked you at eighty-four. That's nineteen miles over the speed limit. I also cited you for wearing headphones. Stop wearing those stupid things, sir. Have a nice day."

I sat there, looking at the little light-yellow paper rectangle in my hand. I knew I had to watch myself. That was dumb move number two. Ticket number two.

The first day off after my father started dialysis felt like the first day of summer vacation. No more studying, no more tests. My dad sat on the couch, half-watching the TV, but I noticed the way he kept looking down at the bandaged fistula on his arm. He felt tired, but not tired enough to keep him from having lunch at his club.

We walked into the lobby. Dad was greeted by one of his gym-rat friends.

"Stan!" he said. "We haven't seen you on the treadmill. Where have you…"

"I'm not going to be there as often, Bob. But I'll get in. I've got some blood cleaning to do."

He pointed to his fistula and walked away.

We headed over to the table. My dad loved going to the club. It was his favorite spot in Peoria. He liked to stop anyone who came near the table for a little chat, just to say hello or give them a story. No long conversations, just a short little burst. He didn't want anything—he wasn't softening them up for the big ask, nothing Machiavellian about his nature. It was just a chance to feel normal when nothing else was. I could tell he was angry, but he still managed to smile at everyone he saw and play at being friendly. He wanted to get back into the gym. The gym had always been his lifeblood.

It was 1972. I had just turned thirteen, and my dad and I were out doing some yardwork. I was in the front yard, raking the pine needles from our neighbor's majestic evergreen. It was a sunny autumn day, and as I warmed up, I took off my thick shirt. My bare arms were sticks—nothing but skin, not even a bone I could pretend was a muscle. I threw down my rake and ran to the backyard, where my dad was raking up leaves from his prized mimosa tree. I looked at him in his T-shirt, muscles bulging beneath, his beefy neck. He looked like Hercules; I looked like Howdy Doody.

"Dad, everyone at school is bigger than me. My arms look like a marionette from Mexico!" I said, thinking of the stick-like puppets my grandmother bought for me whenever she went on her cruises down south. My dad leaned his rake against the mimosa and looked me over.

"Take your shirt off."

"Here? In front of everybody?"

"It's just the mimosa, Steven, and it won't talk. Mr. Mimosa, please look away. See? We are totally private now."

I took my shirt off and stood with my hands on my hips. My dungarees were barely held up by a worn leather belt, and my white Keds looked like clown shoes, oversized and ridiculous beneath my skinny legs.

"I'm not taking off my pants, Dad."

"No need. I can size you up. Let's go upstairs and weigh you."

We walked in through the back door. My mother was at the kitchen table, mixing up a Betty Crocker cake.

"Stanley, he has his shirt off. Are you crazy? It's freezing out there. I'm going to kill you both. Take your shoes off."

We threw our sneakers off and hustled up the stairs two at a time. Barreling into the bathroom, I grabbed the scale from under the sink.

"Make sure each corner is on the grout, so it's even," my dad said. "And take your pants off—I want it exact."

I stood there in my white Fruit of the Looms and watched the arrow spinning this way and that, not registering much at all.

"Eighty pounds," my father said, sitting on the covered toilet seat with his chin in his hand. His muscles looked big even when he was doing nothing. I snuck a peek at the mirror, and it felt like my reflection was mocking me—droopy brown eyes and a frame so skinny it looked like it could be in a commercial begging for donations to help starving kids in Biafra.

"Have you been eating anything but Froot Loops and Jujubes?"

"Dad…" I said, my mouth wrinkling into a frown. Even he knew better.

"I'm just saying, I see you push your food around. There's always half a plate left."

I stared at my toes. I felt horrible.

"Let me check this weight again."

My dad put his thumb on the scale this time, like a deli owner trying to push up his profit.

"Hmm, I was wrong. It's actually eighty-two pounds. You've got some meat on your bones."

"I do?"

"Yep."

But neither of us was really buying it. For a minute, both of us stared down at the black-and-white tiled floor, me moping, and my father thinking. Finally, he reached over and grabbed my bare ankle.

"We are going to put you on a program," he said. "I'll pick up some Joe Weider magazines for inspiration. You're going to start drinking protein shakes, and you're going to work out with me."

I looked up. I couldn't believe my ears. I was going to be included in the secret bastion of our basement, that space my father coveted so highly at the end of the day? Where metal hit the metal? Where the beige tile floor was cracked beneath the weight of the monumental dumbbells?

"I'll get muscles?" I said.

"Oh, you'll get so many muscles, your body will think you live on Mount Olympus."

"Is that upstate?"

"No, it's where the big guys live," my dad said, handing me my pants.

Back down the stairs we bounded, into the kitchen where my mother was putting the cake into the oven.

"Ann, we are going to feed this boy. Steak and potatoes. Vegetables and power shakes. Everything that puts weight and muscle on him."

"What the hell are you talking about? He eats."

73

She slammed the oven door.

"Not like a champion he doesn't. He's going to join the ranks of the body building superstars. I'm building a mean, lean monster."

He explained the plan: We were going to work out together every night. Different body parts each day, different weight levels. Warm up sets, regular sets, super sets.

"And then what?" my mother said, her hands on her hips.

"And then this," my father said, grabbing a nearby muscle magazine. On the cover was the Austrian Oak: Arnold Schwarzenegger. My mother and I were speechless. "Follow me, my boy."

My father had me working out every night after that. Arms, chest, and back on Monday, Wednesday, and Friday. We curled and benched and strained until I couldn't push the iron anymore. Legs on Tuesday, Thursday, and Saturday: running outside, sprints, and sidesteps. Night after night he trained me. I ate mountains of beef, drank gallons of protein shakes, devoured vegetables and salad by the truckload.

My father promised a monster. And in three years, I gained fifty pounds of muscle. My arms were no longer sticks but bricks of flesh. I was built.

And it was my father that did it. No one else—he did it.

My dad cleaned out the blender and handed me a thick chocolate shake.

"Dream, and you can do it, son. Always remember that."

Thursdays were his day off from dialysis. I was thinking about our old workouts when I came into the kitchen; I was missing them. My dad was alone—my sister was food shopping, and my mother was at a lymphedema massage for her left arm, the remnants of her breast cancer. I saw that Dad was finishing his lunch, and I guess I had a moody look on my face.

"Don't take everything seriously, Steven," my dad said to me. "Don't take everything to heart."

He smiled, touched my hand, looked me in the eye, and told me the truth, all with a little laugh. And if it stung, the laugh made it sting a little less.

The phone in my hotel room rang at six a.m., same as always. I moaned and picked it up.

"Dad, I'm shooting nights," I said. "I need to sleep."

"But this is when we always talk, Steven. Are you up?"

"I haven't even been to bed! We shot all night. I'm beat."

"Did you eat breakfast?"

"Yeah, with the guys."

"What's the name of this movie?"

"*Diner*, Dad."

"Well, that sounds right. If they're going to name the movie after a restaurant, might as well eat with the other actors. Tell me about it; I'm doing paperwork."

"Okay, Dad."

I slithered out of the economy hotel bed. It was like sleeping on a slab of concrete. But it didn't matter. No sleep for me—as long as Dad was encouraging me, I had supernatural energy.

When we were filming *Diner*, none of us knew what it was going to be. We couldn't have guessed that *Vanity Fair* was going to one day deem it the most influential film of the last thirty years. To us actors—Paul Reiser, Kevin Bacon, Tim Daly, Danny Stern, Mickey Rourke, and Ellen Barkin—it was a paying job. We were all young, just starting out, doing everything we could to pay the bills.

The movie was shot almost entirely at night, with just a few day scenes. So, we got on a schedule: come to work at five p.m. and leave the set at five a.m. It screwed up our internal clocks, but it also created a creative atmosphere like no other. The world is quiet at two in the morning. All of us were fighting to stay awake. And our brains went into survival mode—we had to kill or be killed. Acting-wise, that is. All of us young and hungry for screen time, wanting to go somewhere we hadn't before.

Luckily, we had Barry Levinson. At two a.m., he was fighting fatigue too, but every night he delivered his best. The six of us actors would share a booth and spar with one another, using the incredible dialogue that Barry gave us. But after we were finished performing what he'd written, he wouldn't say "cut." Instead, he'd wait to see what would happen. And did it ever. The first rule of improvisation is to always say "yes," and "yes" was flying all over the set. Paul Reiser and I did the whole "roast beef" riff as the result of Barry's long leash, letting his young and willing actors play around.

Mickey Rourke and I came to Barry one night in the wee hours, asking for a scene together. We were friends and wanted to do something, just him and I. Barry was delighted by the idea. Maybe there was something between Boogie and Eddie? Maybe a secret?

"What if Steve's Eddie was a virgin, and he exposed that only to you Mickey?"

Mickey's eyes danced the way they did when he got excited. Still very cool, in a way that belongs only to Mickey Rourke. He was our Humphrey Bogart.

So at four in the morning, the rest of the world asleep, Mickey and I waited in our sparse dressing rooms for Barry to knock and tell us he had something. It only took him an hour before we heard a light tapping on Mickey's door.

"Give it a read," Barry said, with a smile that, by then, we knew so well.

There was something about Barry's writing that came through so clearly in that scene—like a song you couldn't get out of your mind. A smoothness like aged whiskey.

"Let's shoot it now, guys."

"Shouldn't we wait 'til we know it by heart, Barry?" Mickey said. He liked to rehearse. "Maybe tomorrow?"

"Nope—now."

It was nearly five in the morning. The other actors had all been let go by the time we staggered onto the set. And Mickey and I started to film the scene where Mickey taught me the meaning of "stealing."

I thought the scene was about me—after all, it was my character making the big admission, telling Boogie I'm a virgin. But on the last take, Mickey picked up a glass sugar holder, poured the contents into his mouth, and washed it down with a Coca Cola. It was like I was invisible. I told my father all about it.

"Here's the deal, Steven," he said. "Every actor should feel lucky if someone steals a scene, even if it's not him. It's like in baseball. If someone on your team steals a base, you have a better shot at winning. That scene made the movie better, I guarantee it."

I heard my father shuffling around some papers.

"That sounds great, Dad. But will anyone even be looking at me in the scene?"

"You were on that celluloid too. Believe me—they'll see you. Now go to sleep."

When I went back to work at five p.m. that day, Barry had already seen the rushes—the rough draft of what the scene would look like in the movie.

"Steve, you're going to like that scene with Mickey. I guarantee it."

He and my dad were both right. Nothing like a scene stealer and being on the field with Mickey. And I was there, on screen, throwing the ball right back. Thanks to Barry and Mickey. And my dad.

Birthdays are a big deal in our family, and Dad loved the hoopla.

I came home, and my brother Joseph and brother-in-law Bob were home to meet me. I had a special surprise for Dad that night.

Chapter SEVEN

The sign for Cabazon stares me in the face. The town is famous for the discount outlet that sprawls there. I've got to stop there sometime, get out and do a little shopping. But my father's birthday beckons, so I resist the urge to exit. I watch a bus full of anxious shoppers get off the exit. I can see the activity in the bus, people pressing their faces against the glass; they look like a high school football team, waiting to get out and play an opponent they know they can take. I wonder, the way I do when I look at almost anyone these days: Do any of them have parents who are compromised?

After the call with my dad, I start looking for the sign for Palm Springs. I can visualize it in my mind: sunny, yellow, and its looping script promising a good time. Every time I drive through, I wonder: Who on earth was able to make Palm Springs? It's in the middle of the Mojave Desert, with no water around for miles, as the crow flies? It's amazing what can be accomplished with a dream, a little greed, and good, old-fashioned know-how. One day I'll go there and lay by a pool, lather on the Hawaiian Tropic. But not today.

The bridge over the freeway announces, "Palm Springs and Other Desert Cities." What a slap in the face for those "other" desert cities. Don't they merit some marquee value? "We like you, Indio, and it was between you and La Quinta, but Palm Springs has the stars, so we're going with Palm Springs." Is everything on this coast a casting opportunity?

Parallel to the freeway, the windmills stand guard. These enormous giants are motionless until the wind picks up. The windmills go on for a few miles; they're a ghostly, unnerving presence.

But machines have begun to take on human characteristics for me. I think dialysis had something to do with that. Because what both the windmills and the dialyzers do is provide. They contribute. But that providing is conditional; it requires watching, maintenance, and attention. I watch the turbines circle, thinking of the dialyzer spinning its blood.

We fell quickly into the routine of dialysis. I learned the rhythms of the week, anticipated what each day would mean for Dad. And for the rest of us too.

There was comfort in the routine. But it left you open too. Because things were always changing.

We walked into the clinic in March 2020, and the lobby was completely different. No chairs next to one another, and the receptionist was behind glass. The passageway to the clinic was locked; we had to be buzzed in. Covid changed everything. Only one of us was allowed into the clinic at a time with my dad. Another tiger in the house. Compromised? G-d damn it, we were compromised. Everyone was wearing masks now. Once we were let into the room, the looks on the techs' faces had changed: more fear, more concern. As if these poor people didn't have enough to deal with. Now this? Damn it.

I sat at the kitchen table with my dad, hoping he would eat enough to carry him through the session. When we started dialysis, we could send him to the clinic with a sandwich and a Boost protein drink. But now that Covid had hit, no more eating. You couldn't take your mask off, not even for a lollypop or a cup of coffee. My father got hungry. And he needed to use the bathroom more, which meant uncoupling from the machine, which meant more time. All those extra hours added up.

I noticed him getting less stoic when he was uncomfortable. He became more vocal—more moaning. It sounded like a howl, and it bothered me. My sister handled it much better than I could.

"I just put a wall around myself," she said, "not letting my emotions in."

But I couldn't do that.

It was a Wednesday. The physical pull on Wednesdays wasn't as harsh on my dad—the toxins had already been grabbed from him on Monday. I quietly opened the door from the garage, not wanting to wake anyone who was sleeping. Mostly, I was thinking about my mother. With all that was going on, she needed her sleep. My dad was sitting in the living room, waiting for me. He had gotten quieter, less chatty as the sessions piled up. We all had.

We still projected the necessary good attitude. It was powerful, being positive. But every so often, we disclosed our sadness to one another. Admitted to crying alone. With every session we saw more, felt it more. Before each dialysis session, we put a numbing agent on the fistula to try and cushion the pain from the stick of the needle. We tried to find our own numbing agents, so we could keep the pain of watching my father go through this all manageable. It was still there, but less sharp.

My mother came into the kitchen and fixed herself a cup of coffee. She poured in a thick ribbon of cream and then wrapped its pitcher in cellophane, to keep it fresh. My sister and Emily loaded up the bag with goodies for *D*—that was what we had taken to calling it, another little numbing agent. My father got more uncomfortable in the pleather chairs; sitting for four hours at a time can wreak havoc on one's derriere. So, we bought cushions from Amazon, Marshalls, Bed Bath and Beyond—anyone who sold booty protectors. It was because my dad was losing weight; it made it harder for him to sit. I did what I could to make him comfy: Werther's hard caramels that he could suck on under the mask, two blankets, special slippers for dialysis, clothing we picked out the night before to make sure the pleather didn't touch his bare skin, a glove for his fistula hand, a pillow for his head, and one of the neck donuts you wear in an airplane. Anything for a little bit of comfort.

The back of my father's head was all I could see as I washed the breakfast dishes. I loaded the sponge with soapy water, cleaned a dish, squeezed out the water, and started again. Squeeze, scrub, clean. As the sponge expanded in the water, I looked at my father's head again, and something occurred to me. He was a sponge. He loaded up on water, fluids, then the fullness was squeezed out of him, and like a sponge, he would spring back. My father the sponge.

He wasn't always like that. I worked hard to remember that.

Police Academy was supposed to be a small movie—the Ladd Company, which was known from movies like *The Right Stuff* and *Once Upon a Time in America*, had basically filmed it as a favor to the producer, Paul Maslansky. He'd been loyal to the company, and they threw him five million bucks to spend seven weeks in Toronto with a bunch of comedians and an actor who'd just come off a modest hit called *Diner*. I thought the movie worked while we were filming in Canada, but tonight was the screening—that would be the real proof of whether my instincts were right.

My manager, Sandy Gallin, was coming with me to watch it for the first time. He was a tough critic and a top manager, known for handling other talent like Whoopi Goldberg and Dolly Parton. He picked me up in his Bentley, and we flew down Sunset Boulevard, left on Laurel Canyon, and right on Ventura, until we got to Warner Brothers Studios.

"This better be good, Steven," he said as we drove. "I could be at David Geffin's house instead of watching a maybe baby."

"I guarantee it's good, Sandy. I laughed the whole time we shot it."

Sandy turned to me with a face like a skull: no emotion at all.

"Roll it, Leo," he said to the projectionist.

The lights went out, and on screen appeared some young people on their first day of police training. The music roared, a happy, military-inflected tune that played over the titles. After ten minutes of uproarious laughter from me, I looked at Sandy—he looked totally nonplussed. As the movie kept playing, I could hear the projectionist laughing, along with a few stragglers in the back.

The movie ended, and I was on cloud nine. I'd laughed 'til my face hurt. I asked Sandy what he thought.

"This is the biggest piece of shit I've ever seen," he said on his way out to the parking lot. "I'm sticking you in a TV series, pronto."

As soon as I got back home, I called my dad.

"Steven, it's one in the morning here. How'd the screening go?"

"It's a bomb, Dad. They're going to put me in a TV series."

"Well, I like TV. I like Phil Silvers. He didn't do too bad."

"I want to be a movie star, Dad."

"Tell you what. When you do a TV show, I'll come out there. I think it's good."

True to his word, Sandy got me a pilot the very next day after the screening. A good one too: *The Ferret*, starring Robert Loggia, Sam Wanamaker, and Brian Dennehy. Directed by the great Blake Edwards. They had been looking for a co-lead, and there I was. Shooting was set to start in a week.

"*The Pink Panther*'s Blake Edwards?" my dad said when I told him the news. He was a huge Julie Andrews fan, and he still couldn't get over Julie doing the nude scene in *S.O.B.*

"Steven, when I get out there, I'm going to ask Mr. Edwards why he would let his wife go topless for all the world to see. I wouldn't let your mother wear a low-cut top, much less show her private lady parts to the world."

I heard my mother in the background.

"Stanley, hang up! It's the middle of the night, and who are you talking to about my lady parts?"

"Steven," my dad said, "I'll call you in the morning."

At six a.m. on the dot, like always, my phone rang again.

"I made a reservation. I'm coming out next week. Then you and I can talk to Mr. Edwards about the nudity, and you can shoot your pilot. Why do they call it a pilot, anyway? Are you flying somewhere with it?"

"I don't know, Dad."

"Another question for Mr. Blake Edwards when we see him."

That day, I drove to Blake Edwards's office in Brentwood. He had a private dining room in his office—and a private chef. I'd never seen that before. Lunch was just the two of us and Tony Adams, the president of his company. Tony had been Mr. Edwards's driver at some point, and now he ran the whole company. We dined on leg of lamb, blackberry jam, and vegetables grown in Julie Andrews's home garden. After lunch, Blake Edwards handed me the script.

"You start shooting in two days," he said. "I need you letter perfect—Loggia is a real stickler."

I didn't leave my house again until I had to go to the airport to pick up my dad. It was four in the afternoon; my first call time was that night at seven. I waited at the gate until my dad came trotting up to me.

"You look tan," he said. "Do you have makeup on?"

"I haven't even been out of the house for twenty-four hours—I've been working on this script."

"Well, we better check your blood pressure. Speaking of—do you think I'll get to meet Julie Andrews?"

"I don't know, Dad. You sure won't meet her topless, if that's what you're thinking."

My dad looked at me hard for a second—that was all it took.

"Sorry. That was disrespectful."

"It was, Steven, but not a big deal. You've just been out in Hollywood-land too long."

We pulled up to the set early. Trucks were parked all over, and some of the crew were milling about by the catering truck. A second assistant director flagged me over.

"Blake said to put you in the big trailer," he said. He looked over at my father. "This your brother?"

I thought my father was going to burst his buttons.

"I'm his dad," he said.

"His dad? Man, you look like a young stuntman."

We walked into the trailer, and as my father closed the door behind him, he looked at me and let out a whoop.

"I'm a young stuntman! Can you believe it? See, working out has its benefits!"

By the time we left the trailer for the shoot, it had started to get cold. It'd been eighty-five degrees during the day—neither of us had brought a jacket—and my father looked at me.

"What happened to the warm California weather?"

"It hides like a coward in the night, Dad."

My father had been an Airborne Ranger—he knew the difference between a coward and a brave man.

"Hiding isn't cowardly, Steven. Sometimes—often—it's smart."

"Well then, California nights must be geniuses, Dad."

Blake Edwards was already on set when we arrived, dressed like a fashion icon in a large chair with "Director" stenciled on it.

"Great to see you," he said, before laying out the first shot—a stunt. "You stand up there, about thirty feet up—you'll have a rig on—and jump onto this airbag. Two stuntmen will use the ropes to slow down the speed of your fall, and you'll land on this giant stunt pillow. Piece of cake!"

My face, apparently, suggested that this might not be a piece of cake for me.

"What's wrong?" he said. "Can't do it?"

I knew this man was a legend. He had directed *Breakfast at Tiffany's*—one of my favorite films. I didn't want to disappoint him on my first day, my first stunt, the first shot.

"I'll do it, Mr. Edwards," said my dad. "I'll try it out for Steven, and if it's safe, as I'm sure it is, he'll do it after. Deal?"

"Mr. Guttenberg, have you ever jumped from thirty feet?"

"No, I haven't."

Everyone, including Mr. Edwards, sighed.

"But I have jumped from fifteen hundred feet. I'm a Ranger."

"An Airborne Ranger?"

"Eighty-second."

Mr. Edwards smiled wide.

"Then who else would we want testing it out?"

My dad had only one request—hot coffee, black.

"It's freezing here in California," he said. "Now I know why Sinatra sang, 'The lady doesn't like California, it's cold and it's damp.'"

My dad and Mr. Edwards smiled as two stuntmen started to put my dad in the rig. I looked like a puppy in a rainstorm.

"Maybe I should do it," I said. "It is my part in the show."

"Not on your life, son. It'll be fun for me. If it's safe, then you can do it too. And if it isn't, then your mother will be a rich woman from the insurance."

"Dad, that's not funny!"

"Besides, maybe Julie Andrews will show up, and I can meet her."

"Julie Andrews isn't coming to a night shoot. I'll buy you a pizza."

"A guy can dream, can't he?" my dad said.

A few of the stuntmen led my dad up to the tower. When Dad got to the top, he yelled down, "This is more than thirty feet, Mr. Edwards."

"No, Stanley, it's thirty!"

Joe Dunne, the stunt coordinator, walked over.

"Actually Blake, it's fifty feet in the air. It's the only way the fall would appear real."

"Oh. Sorry, Stanley, it's fifty, I apologize."

"No problem, Blake. More time for me to relax on the way down."

I started to sweat, the way I do when I'm nervous, even in the cold.

"Dad, you don't have to do this!"

Just then, a Rolls-Royce pulled up to the set. The door opened, and out stepped Mary Poppins herself: Julie Andrews. She walked up to Blake and kissed him on the cheek.

"Whatcha all doing?"

"A stunt, honey," Mr. Edwards said. "Want to go to the trailer?"

"Not on your life, Blake. That man looks like he's a hundred feet up! Is it Joe Dunne up there?"

"Not me, Dame Andrews," Joe said. "It's this young actor's father. He's trying it out for his son."

"Well, that's brave."

She couldn't take her eyes off Dad.

"You ready, Mr. Guttenberg?" Joe said.

"I sure am," he yelled. Then, a moment later, "Is that Julie Andrews down there?"

My dad had eyes like a hawk.

"'Tis me, Mr. Guttenberg!"

I could see Blake wince. Jealousy? Nah, couldn't be!

"Then this is for you, Miss von Trapp!"

Joe counted it down and yelled, "Jump!"

My dad did a perfect swan dive, followed by a somersault, into the stunt pillow. He dismounted like a trapeze artist and took a minute to catch his breath. There was a round of applause as he headed towards the camera. The first to hug him was Blake Edwards. The second was Julie Andrews.

"We call that showboating, Walton-on-Thames-style, Mr. Guttenberg," Julie Andrews said. There was a giggle in her voice.

"We call that having a little fun, Brooklyn-style, Ms. Andrews."

I thought he was going to faint when she hugged him.

I did the stunt after my dad. And as we walked back to the trailer to get ready for my next scene, Dad stopped me and laughed.

"Julie Andrews came to a night shoot, and I met her. I'll take my pizza half-sausage, half-pepperoni. Pronto."

We had fun, my dad and I.

It was the tail end of June 1968; the air was starting to get humid. Fourth grade was ending, and I could feel the three months of delirium that was coming.

And I was ready. Because I'd been collecting. I had enough fireworks to last the whole summer. I took every penny I made from my *Newsday* delivery route and poured them into "belts," these macho configurations of 144 firecrackers. These particular belts came straight from China, with Chinese calligraphy on the wrapper, and to my young perspective, they were the ultimate asset. Better than gold.

I bought belt after belt from Andy Mahoney, who was notorious in my neighborhood for lighting my neighbor's garage on fire with a chlorine bomb. He was an anti-hero, a rebel with a cause, five years older than I was. The only reason he talked with me was because I was buying from him.

Initially I kept all that gunpowder in the ingenious hideaway I'd devised: the side drawer of my desk. By some miracle, my mother never found them. But they couldn't just sit in that drawer forever; I had to see if they would work.

So I decided to get a pack of matches, lock myself in the family bathroom, and throw lit firecrackers out the only window. My father was down in the den, my mother in the kitchen. How could I possibly get caught? I proceeded to create my own personal preview of the Fourth of July.

And wouldn't you know it? Someone noticed.

"What the hell is going on?" I heard my mother say downstairs. "Stanley, I smell smoke."

"Check the air conditioners," my father said. "I'm going to look at the attic."

I heard my father's footsteps as he rushed up to the attic, praying that he would skip past the bathroom I'd turned into my private gunpowder studio. But then he started banging on the door.

"Steven? What the hell are you doing in there?"

"Nothing," I said, my voice extremely calm.

I dropped another lit belt out the window.

"Open this door, *now!*"

I looked around the family bathroom: Where could I hide these suckers? Where could I hide myself? Nowhere seemed promising. So, after a moment, I opened the door.

A plume of smoke billowed out into the rest of the house. I was covered in soot. My father looked me over, and as he stood there for what felt like a very long time, I was sure he was going to hand me my head. And not on a platter.

"I'll tell you what I'm going to do," he said. I started to sweat. "How many firecrackers do you have?"

I went to my trusty desk drawer and slid it open. He was the only human to ever see that cache—other than Andy Mahoney.

"That's a lot of gunpowder. How did you get all these firecrackers?"

"They're called belts, Dad," I said. He raised his eyebrows—not the right answer. "I got them using my newspaper route money."

He reached into the drawer and, with one giant hand, grabbed the bulk of them.

"Follow me."

We headed outside. I was sure that we were going to the garbage pails, but he walked right past them.

"You and me are going to light every firecracker in these belts and finish them off."

I was going to light firecrackers with my father? These were contraband, but he—an ex-cop—was willing to put himself in harm's way for me? That's a dad. That's a father.

We stood on the patio, and as the sun started to set, we handed each other single cylinders of gunpowder. My father had his Zippo lighter—he lit each one carefully and then threw it onto the lawn. *Pow! Bang!* My dad was lighting firecrackers, and it made me delirious. I carefully twisted a cracker off the belt, handed it to my dad, barrel first, and within seconds it had exploded into a green cloud of smithereens.

Then my father started to get creative—he'd light the firecrackers and then throw them high so they'd explode in mid-air, nipping the edge of the mimosa tree. After a time, he turned to me.

"Here, you light some," he said. "I've got an extra Zippo."

I started slow, lighting the wick and then running as I dropped them on the ground. But I saw my father's confidence and started to throw them onto the lawn too. Dad threw one. I threw one. Our explosions echoing one another: call and response, question and answer.

"What the hell are you two doing?" my mother said, her head halfway out the bedroom window.

"We're lighting firecrackers, Ann. My partner and me."

His partner. Dad called me his partner. It was like I'd joined the Yankees and the Mets all at once.

There we stood, for hours, as the sun set over the mimosa tree. I looked up at my dad: my hero, my partner. We lit every last one. Of course, one blew up between my fingers; the pain was spectacular, but I didn't dare tell. This was too good.

It was dark as we lit the last few. They unwrapped and exploded in the air, illuminating the backyard with blasts of light.

"That's it, Steven. We're done. Good job."

I walked back into the house a little changed. A little more trust from my dad. A little bit more like a man.

I brought Dad to a big-time premiere in New York City. It was an action pic so we dressed casually, but the studio sent a limo to Massapequa.

I came to Hollywood with $300 my folks gave me for food and telephone calls, and years later, with my parents' belief in me, I was able to surprise them with a house I bought in LA. Their eyes were wide as saucers—they were just over the moon.

Chapter EIGHT

From the freeway, all I can see are fast food restaurants. Home cooking is gone. But I can still remember the corner store—the neighborhood joint that wasn't a chain. And they were packed. My dad and I loved places like that: diners and delis, pizza shops and luncheonettes. Run by real people, owners who cared about their customers. I yearn for the days when he and I would go grab a hot dog or a pastrami sandwich. There was nothing like a counter filled with working people grabbing a bit on their lunch break—the simple enjoyment of being elbow to elbow with strangers. Dad loved starting conversations. He loved a quick chat, and the stories he could tell in only a few minutes would stay with people forever. And then, the next time we sat at that counter, a now-familiar face would sidle up and order a tuna melt.

"Hey, Stan," he'd say. "I've been thinking about that story you told about the tanks coming through your outfit in Korea."

But there's none of that out here on the 10. Just chains, for as far as the eye can see.

I'm staring out the side window at a woman in the next lane putting on her makeup and two kids in the back seat playing with computer games. She has coffee on the dashboard, and in between applications of lipstick and eyeliner, she's feeding the kids eggs from a Styrofoam tray.

Flushing again—in that two-bedroom Queens apartment. I was five, maybe six. It was summer and hot as hell without air conditioning. My mother had all the windows open, but the only thing that came in was thick, dank air. She ran the water cold and wet a dishrag to keep around her neck. She was breathing hard and lit up a cigarette.

"I'm hungry, Ma," I said.

"I just fed you. And you left everything on your plate."

"There's nothing to do."

This complaint particularly rankled my mother. My parents had saved up to send me to camp—a day camp with arts and crafts, swimming, lunch, and lots of other kids. But the second day the bus came to pick me up, I hid in the apartment. I had no interest in completing the lanyard keychain I'd started or having anything else to do with the camp.

So, from that day on, my mother and I were together day and night. And I was a nut. I veered back and forth from exciting and entertaining one minute to depressed and bored the next. And I wouldn't let her have a moment of peace.

"I wish you went to camp, Steven. There's lots to do—better than sitting around this hot apartment."

She took a long drag of her cigarette.

"Ma… Ma… Ma…"

"What?"

"I don't know. What do I do?"

"Bang your head against the wall."

I followed her around the house, asking for things she couldn't do and questions that had no answers, until finally she would start to cry from sheer exhaustion with me.

"Ma, I have no friends. Ma, where are my old toys? Ma, you're not playing with me!"

"Steven, please, here's your coloring book."

"I don't want it."

"Here's the TV—watch a show."

"No. Ma, I'm bored. I have nothing to do."

She was a young woman, alone in that apartment with a maniac. Money was tight and her husband was at work. She had moved from Brooklyn and had few friends in Queens. My sister Judi was crying in her crib, and she was pregnant with my sister Susan, nauseous all day.

I just wouldn't let up on her until finally she just sat on her knees and cried. Sobs. She couldn't catch her breath. I just watched her. She couldn't stop weeping.

"Steven…I…can't…do this anymore with…you. Please. I can't. It's just too much."

She picked up the phone and called my father. Then, for a little while, there was silence. Even at that age, I could see what I had done—the way I'd brought that tiny world of the apartment crashing down around her. But now I couldn't help her. I couldn't turn back time. No way to take back the pain I had caused. The best I could do was to shut up for a little while.

An hour passed. My mother just sat on the bed, staring out the window, probably thinking about a different life. Eventually the door opened, and my father rushed to her, holding her in his arms.

"Ann, Ann."

"Dad, I didn't do anything."

"Go to the other room. Go see your sister. You can't do this to your mother."

He held my mom with such tenderness—that was him. But he never punished me for that.

But don't be fooled—my mother was a very strong lady. Brooklyn blood. And she had been through a great deal. She lost her father young. The two of them were close—soul close. My father said that when Grandpa Sam died, my mother came into their apartment and wouldn't let him go as the paramedics took him out. When she left, Grandma Kate followed them to the elevator, and my mom turned to her.

"I'm never going to love anyone this much again," my mom said.

She told me that after her father had his first heart attack, he started to distance himself from her. As if he knew that he was going to go and didn't want her to miss him. My grandfather was a longshoreman—I still have the hook he used to grapple ships' cargo hanging in my office. Touching that tool, it's like I can feel the sinews of his arms, the way he physically grabbed for one of the few available jobs—for the promise of eating, paying rent, and taking care of your family; the turn of your stomach when you didn't come home with any green; and being man enough to somehow keep that pressure to yourself.

The hook sits in my office next to my great-grandfather's linoleum knife. Both are still sharp as hell. The tools of men whose wives were devoted to them.

It was January 2000. The world was supposed to have folded up, with the computers headed for catastrophic collapse. But they didn't. Life continued, and Y2K was just a hoax.

We were in Boca Raton Hospital, waiting in the pre-op area. I watched my mother look at her husband, her lover, her man—her everything. He was the oak tree we all lived under. The stark white walls of the hospital provided little comfort and no warmth. My father was scheduled to have his rib cage cracked, his heart removed and rested on his chest while the surgeons bypassed the arteries.

It took a mental shift to see my dad vulnerable. And it seemed to take my mom far away from those hospital walls. We three kids held her as my dad was being wheeled in, but my mother made sure she was the last to kiss him.

"Let me be with my husband."

I had never heard my mom call Dad her husband in such steel tones. He was our father. But after all the fights, all the disagreements, all the terse words over the years, her message was clear—kids, back off. Proprietary.

"He's my husband."

She said it like it was something holy. And what a fool I was—of course it was holy. That bond is holy.

Time *to* Thank

We sat in that hospital for ten days. The clouds parted on the day we drove him home. But still, we knew now that there was a chink in his armor that hadn't been there before.

Long Island. Summer again, July. I was eight years old, and even though it was only seven thirty at night, the sky was dark with heavy rain clouds. I could hear thunder, and the wind—warm just an hour earlier—had abruptly turned cold. Clouds gathered in a dark ball and sat above our apartment building.

I was coming back from playing ring-a-levio with the neighborhood kids. I leaned my bike up against the bricks of the house. And then I heard it: a rager. My mother and father were arguing. There had been many that summer, and I knew they were about me. They were fighting because I was having trouble getting used to the new neighborhood, the new school, the new kids. I was sure no one liked me, and I wanted to go back to Flushing. I wanted to live on busy streets with strollers and noise, smell people cooking dinner in their apartments as I went up to ours, and feel the excitement of the crime that was encroaching every building on Franklin Avenue.

It was only years later that I realized that my parents' arguments had nothing to do with me. They had their own adjustments to deal with. I gingerly walked through the backyard and up the wooden steps to the kitchen door. And there were my parents, at odds with each other. I opened the screen door.

"Steven, go upstairs and wash up for bed."

"But, Mom, I…"

"Steven, do what your mother said."

My father looked awful: his face contorted and strained. I walked reluctantly up the stairs, listening to their whispers. And then my father slammed his hand down on the table. That big, soft hand.

He ran up the stairs behind me and grabbed his leather jacket.

"Where are you going?" I asked, even though I knew he was getting in the car—I'd seen it before.

"Just out for some air. No big deal. Go to bed—I'll see you tomorrow."

I watched from my window as he got in the Dodge Dart, slammed the door behind him, and drove down the street, passing under the wide, open embrace of the old neighborhood oak tree. Just red tail-lights in the night.

Winter now. December 15, 2005—I was home for a few days for the holidays, eating up the family time. My sister Susan and I had gotten especially close—she reminded me so much of my dad. We went holiday shopping at the mammoth Roosevelt Field mall, feeling high on running here and there with the Christmas music blaring. We were like kids again, eating all the junk food, playing pranks on each other with Santa hats. It felt like the Christmas music even followed us out to the parking lot. We laughed as we escaped the cold and settled into my sister's Jeep.

Then her phone rang. Her smile went blank as she held the phone to her ear, and then a tear ran down her cheek.

"What? Susan, what is it?"

My sister couldn't speak. She hung up the phone and collapsed against the steering wheel.

My mother had breast cancer.

It was a punch to the face. It changed me. Even the word sucks. That hard *C* and slithering *ess* pronunciation. It elevated everything in a dark way: your blood pressure, heart rate, the acid in your stomach. It planed my skin, cutting off a layer each time I heard it.

Devotion helped numb that pain, to an extent. But the pain was still there, like a Post-it note glommed onto my skull—I saw it every day, every hour, every minute. The everyday smiles were muted; feelings I used to have pure and clear were now muddied and granular. Nothing tasted as good as it used to. Music didn't sound the same. The air and sunshine didn't embrace me like they had before. There was a devil in our house now, and as long as it roamed, there was something weighing on my spine. I couldn't shake it.

My mother's mastectomy was a shock for her. But it was very hard for both of my parents. They're connected by those unseen threads reverberating between them. What she feels, so does he.

Time *to* Thank

My father was strong: he stood up through the surgery, through the radiation, through all the pain my mother endured. But it wore on them, the constant pressure of the disease. We three children accompanied them, but it was different for my parents, behind closed doors, as close to that tiger as you can get.

My mother had a piece of skin, as big as two inches around, that just wouldn't close after her surgery. It sat under her arm like a waiting enemy. She was undone by it, and so were we. The plastic surgeon who worked with Mom could stitch it up—and he tried, many times. But it just wouldn't close. It was ever present, never letting her forget her amputation, or her disease.

A colleague and friend of mine, Stephen Wetzel, suggested a barometric pressure chamber—the same ones used to "de-bend" scuba divers when they come up too quickly. Athletes use the chambers too, to repair ripped tendons and ligaments. And, as it turned out, they are also used for wound repair. We didn't know that, and the surgeon didn't know about it either, which was hard to believe, but true. So, we went on a hunt for a barometric pressure chamber on Long Island. The only one resided at Nassau Hospital, famous for shootings and super max violent criminals. On our first visit, we saw handcuffed arm after handcuffed arm on our way to the barometric department.

It took sixty long days, three to four hours a day. My mother lay in this chamber on 100 percent oxygen. The theory was that the oxygen would speed the healing process. Day after day we sat there, my father watching his wife while she watched movies, tried to sleep, and waited for the end of the session.

Slowly—frustratingly slow—the hole began to close. It shrank to the size of a quarter, and then a nickel, and then a dime. And after sixty days, it closed. And through it all, my father sat by his wife. Just as she sat by her husband as he started dialysis.

This part of life, it's just hard as hell. But my parents are tough.

It was January 1974, and we were in the middle of one of the coldest winters in the history of Long Island. It was six thirty in the morning, and my father was out front, shoveling snow—up to four feet high, with the wind drifts. I was sixteen years old and had no interest in anything that involved getting out of bed.

"Get up," my father said, already wearing his full winter regalia: hat, gloves, parka, scarf, and waterproof rubber pants. He was sweating and soaked with flecks of ice. "I need help out front with the snow."

"I'm up," I said. "I'll be out in a minute."

"You better be. Your mom is on the warpath."

He struggled to move under all his layers as he trundled back down the stairs, giving me one last look as he went. I could hear his heavy steps as he headed back outside. But I had no intention of getting up and shoveling snow. Not a chance.

A little while later, I heard the creak of my parents' bedroom door and the familiar sound of my mother's bare feet against the floor. Then, nothing. I hid my eyes under the covers, knowing my mother was now in my bedroom doorway.

"Steven, your father asked you to help him shovel the friggin' snow. Get up."

"I will, Ma. Just a minute more."

I turned over in my warm-as-toast-on-a-Sunday-morning bed. She came over to the side of my bed, where my father had stood a few minutes before.

"Darling. I need you to get up now. Please, sweetheart?"

I knew something was amiss when she asked nicely. I turned over, and there before me was the most outlandish cartoon version of the woman I'd ever seen. Her hair looked like she'd been through a hurricane, her housecoat was crumpled and two sizes too big, and she had no makeup on.

"Ann, is he up?" my father yelled in through the half-open front storm door.

"Honey, can you go help your father?"

I just started to laugh. And with that,

"Mom, you look too funny! Seriously, Ma, I'll do it later."

"Steven," my father called up. "She's going to kill you. Get down here."

But I just couldn't get over her appearance. And, like a true teenager with nothing inside his brain, I kept laughing.

"Think it's funny?"

"Yeah, Ma, I do."

"Well…"

And with that, she stood me up—she was strong, surprisingly strong—pulled me to the front door and tossed me out in just my cotton pajamas.

"He's all yours. He can shovel now."

My dad, laughing, took off his long winter coat and handed it to me.

"Better put this on, son, or I'll have to cut off your frostbitten extremities with this shovel."

My dad leaned on his shovel. I noticed now just how sharp the edge really was.

I went and knocked on the door.

"Ma, come on, joke's over. Let me in."

Her face was much cuter now as her nose and eyes peered out of the glass window.

"No, you're not coming back in. You're going to stay out there and freeze your nuts off. Good luck!"

My dad laughed and laughed. My sisters called down taunts from their bedroom. I ran to the back porch—there was a cup of hot tea waiting for me.

"Drink your tea, sonny boy," my mother yelled from inside. "And shovel that snow!"

I shoveled the snow until my mother thought I'd learned my lesson. Even with my dad's parka, my pajama legs froze.

I never stayed in bed again!

Another Thursday in Peoria, Arizona. I came into the house, and dinner was on the stove. I thought back to that day in the snow—how long ago now?

My father was at his usual perch on the couch. It was his day off from dialysis. He was cold; I covered him with two blankets. He wanted to talk logistics.

"After dinner, I'm going to get in my pajamas and get in bed. I've got dialysis tomorrow. Who's taking me?"

I kissed his cheek.

"Me, Dad."

"We leave at ten. And we're bringing sandwiches for Christmas."

"I know. I'll be here."

I put my arm around him, trying to warm him up. I picked up the sweatshirt around the back of his neck.

"Dinner's ready," my mom called from the other room. She saw me trying to help him to the table. "You can get up, Stanley. You don't need Steven."

He slowly rose from the couch and grabbed his walker. We made our grudging way to the table. We ate in silence, mostly—he wasn't hungry. But he ate a little ice cream after dinner, and after another rest on the couch, we walked together to the bedroom. He sat on the bed while we discussed different pajama options.

"You want the blue ones? Or the stripes?"

"I don't care. I'm just wearing the bottoms. I want to wear this T-shirt. I only put it on for dinner."

The day pants slipped off, along with his underwear. Susan had told me to let him put his own clothes on—it helped him keep his dexterity, she said. But I liked to help him. I thought it was worth sacrificing a little dexterity practice for comfort.

His legs were skinny. No matter how often I saw his thin frame, it bothered me. He was such a strapping man—he worked out all his life, pumping iron at twelve in a friend's apartment and disturbing the neighbors downstairs with the banging of weights on the floor. He was the man who won the "skin the cat" calisthenics contest at Pershing High School. Concrete muscles and a sense of balance allowed him to do handstands whenever he liked, to the delight of the crowd—to the delight of those he loved. Now my legs were thicker than his. We had traded places in form, and I didn't like it.

I sat next to him, and he laid back, his torso next to me. I put my arm around him, and he snuggled in. And then, after a moment, he began to say, "Oh, Steven, I miss you. I miss you."

I just listened, not knowing what to do or say but dying a little inside.

"I'm sorry, Steven. I could just cry. I miss you. I miss you."

Was this a little dementia? Or was this really how he felt? But I was there. I only spent a few days back in LA, getting my business done. Is that what he meant?

But then, as soon as it had started, it was over.

"Can you get me some yogurt?" he said. "There's an open one in the refrigerator."

Because of my dad's thinning esophagus, he had to take his nighttime pills with yogurt. We didn't want too much liquid going into him.

"Sure, Dad," I said.

I wanted my ol' dad back.

My dad constantly wanted me to stop "paparazzi-ing" him. "Enough with the photos, Steven!"

For my parents' 50th anniversary, we flew to Italy for three weeks. My mom had never been to Europe, and my dad knew it from his years in the service. All my dad wanted was to show Mom "his Europe."

Chapter NINE

On the horizon, I see an outpost in the middle of the Mojave Desert. Nothing around for miles except the desert rats in their small tents and campers on the way out, slipping away from civilization. I've begun looking forward to this stop as the desert sand crunches against the treads of the Kia's tires: the Chiriaco Summit Café and Museums. It's almost exactly halfway between where I started and where I'm going, and I'm going to take a few moments to wolf down some breakfast.

I put on my windshield wipers as I get off the long exit, trying to get off the bugs and the grit I've accumulated so far. There's a tank parked nearby, its US Army star faded but still proud and its barrel pointed straight at me. There's a whole grouping of old war machines off in the distance: M3 half-tracks, jeeps, artillery guns, and turrets. Once violent and dangerous bits of metal are now relegated to photo ops for the civilians who choose the General Patton Memorial Museum over a snow cone. I pull into the lot and park beneath a larger-than-life statue of General Patton and his trusty war dog, Willie.

I run into the café, hoping to get a seat at the counter. It's packed, as usual—how can there be this many people looking to eat when I see so few others on the road? But one patron makes a move to exit and I grab the stool, still warm from his buns. Marla comes over. She's my favorite waitress, a descendant of the original Chiriaco family that built all this out of sand and sweat in the middle of a 110-degree desert. There was nothing here but tumbleweeds and rattlesnakes, and they built a respite for the haggard traveler to wet his whistle, have some ham and eggs, and fill up on gas. They dug down far enough to build a cold metal case to keep provisions cool, and built a dream.

Marla has my food ready quickly, the way I hoped she would—she always comes through. I grab some of their famous hot sauce and think about the museum. No time to visit it today—I'm on a mission—but I've stopped often enough that even the ham and eggs reminds me of the general. Patton was a California boy. He housed his troops here in the Mojave, preparing them for the blistering, unforgiving heat of the North African theater. They used plenty of live ammunition for their training (try keeping gunpowder cool and calm in the unshaded sun). The ground baked. Nothing could be worse than the Mojave in the summer. But he created a world for his men and women and sent them off to war with swagger.

Patriotism runs a little feverish here. I think of my dad, and his decision to enlist instead of waiting to be drafted, and then training as a Ranger. The adventure of his young life: walking out of the hospital where his mother lay with a ravaging disease to go join the Army because he had a sense his country needed him. To be sent off to lands he could only imagine. The turmoil of it all. That took real balls.

I head back out to the parking lot. My Kia is parked next to a US Army jeep, circa 1953. It's the same vehicle my father drove. I can see him sitting in the front seat, one arm on the wheel, the other hanging off the door, and a smile around the cigarette in his mouth.

The gas gauge winks at me: half full. I go over to the pump to top it off.

When I started driving as a teen, my father told me, "When the arrow says half, fill it up. Don't take chances, Steven. Educated chances, yes. But seat-of-your-pants chances are often illusions, and then you find yourself on the side of the road, looking for someone to take you home. Always make sure you have enough. Top it off. You don't want to be caught with your pants down."

I always try to follow his advice: double-check the stove is off and make sure I have directions before I leave the house. Money in one pocket, my phone in the other. But how many times did I have to come running back into the house for something, passing my dad sitting on the couch as I sprinted back up to the bedroom?

"Forgot my wallet!"

"I know," he would say, shaking his head. He wanted me to have the lesson tattooed on my brain. *Top it off.*

Summer, 1973. Saturday morning. I was fifteen years old, and all I wanted to do was drive.

I'd been asking my dad for months to let me try my hand behind the wheel. And that morning, when he told me he was going into the office, I tried again, not expecting the answer to be any different.

"Can I drive, Dad?"

There was my father, filling up the doorway to my bedroom with his strong silhouette. He looked at me with those dark eyes.

"Yes. But don't tell your mother."

I couldn't believe it! I flew down the stairs, landed with a bang loud enough to attract my mother's attention.

"What the hell is going on?" she called from the kitchen. I poked my head in—she was down on her hands and knees, washing the floor.

"I'm going into work with Dad."

"He's not driving, is he, Stanley?" she said.

My father came in, his hand up to the light in the hallway to keep it from nicking his skull.

"Not until he gets his permit," he said. "We'll be back soon. I'll pick up some Carvel."

And then my father winked at me. Actually winked. He had never done that before. He wasn't a clubby kind of guy, the sort who keeps secrets, hides things from his wife. But now we had this between us.

We got into the car, and my father drove on Boundary Avenue, heading to the Oyster Bay Expressway—the fastest road in town. I suddenly had a vision of him putting me behind the wheel there, like throwing a kid into the deep end of the pool to teach them how to swim. But just as I really started to sweat, he eased into a right turn, breezed down to the Jericho Turnpike, and headed to the industrial park where he had an office.

The windows were rolled down, and I could smell the honeysuckle along the side wall of the building. There's nowhere more like summer than Long Island.

"Okay, slide over."

My father got out and hopped over the hood to the passenger's side. I scooched into the driver's seat, staring at the dashboard and the steering wheel.

"Put on your safety belt and start the car. And don't tell your mother."

This was our secret, my father and me. Every Saturday we went to the industrial park and drove around the brand-new blacktop. Eventually, I graduated to moving in and out of the neighborhood driveways, and then finally parallel parking. That took me way too long to master, but it didn't seem to bother my dad.

After an hour, we would go into his office so he could put in a little work before we went back home.

I would sit there, still glowing from being behind the wheel. I miss our secrets. Although we still have a few between us.

When it got too cold in the dialysis center, I smuggled in a heating pad. It was against the rules at the center, and I knew I would get caught eventually. But my father got so cold, sitting there in his dialysis chair, that I figured it was worth the risk. I'd take a chance to give him some momentary relief. The key was to stash the heating pad between two of the dialysis center blankets, branded with the name of the center. I wrapped the pad around his legs, turned it up to the third notch, and prayed that this wouldn't be the day that somebody noticed and told me it wasn't allowed.

One night, out in Arizona, my dad turned to me.

"Steven, I want to take a shower."

Have you ever showered with your father to make sure he was okay? *Sigh*. It was a revelation.

My job was to make sure he didn't fall. I stripped down and put on a bathing suit. We turned on the water.

"Make sure it's not too hot or too cold," my mother said from the other side of the bathroom door.

"I got it, Ma," I said. "The water's nice."

"It's nice, Ann!" my dad called out. Then he looked back at me. "Soap up my hair, Steven."

My father, still in charge. I shampooed his hair—there was something comforting about the soft feeling of his hair beneath my fingers. I washed the soap off his back and then gave him the washcloth so he could scrub his privates.

We joked around the whole time; it made it easier. The "schmooze" helped both of us. But the whole time I was just focused on making sure he didn't fall. My giant dad now had a skinny behind but kept those still-strong hands. When I wasn't in Arizona, or couldn't do it, my mom or Susan would watch him, diverting their eyes as best they could while making sure he was still safe.

His skinny body still bothered me. But still—he had that firm grip, reminding me who he really was.

Saturday afternoon, after dialysis. The sun was shining across my father's shoulders and onto the documents he'd brought with him into bed. He was in his pajamas; he loved doing his paperwork in bed.

I can still remember being back in the one-bedroom apartment in Flushing, and my dad calling me over to the two adjoining single mattresses that made up the bed he shared with my mother. The flower and bumblebee bedspread was covered in important and sophisticated documents: bills and notices, business letters, and receipts from every store in the neighborhood.

"Sit here on the edge," he said to me. "And be quiet, but watch. Paperwork is important."

I sat while my father filled out every check for the bills. I noticed that the checks had his name printed right there in the top corner.

"Dad, if our name is on those checks, we must be pretty important."

He looked up from the papers and smiled at me.

"We are, son. We are an important family."

I watched the script he wrote, carefully and professionally, on the long line in the middle of the checks. His writing was so beautiful. And his signature was like a piece of art: straight and even, like a fancy department store sign, or something out of the opening credits of the movies. I was becoming aware that there was a whole world of writing beyond the block printing I was learning in kindergarten.

"What kind of writing is that?"

"It's called script, or cursive."

"Cursing? Like in bad words?"

My crew cut stood on end.

"No, not bad words. Actually, good words. This is how adults— big boys—write. Want to learn how to write your name in script?"

"In cursive?"

"Yes. Come here, come next to me."

I jumped up on the bed in a single leap, and if it wasn't for my dad's fast hands, there would have been a bookkeeping catastrophe. He swept a space for me on the bedspread, took my hand, and fitted the Paper Mate into it. And then he and I wrote out my name, in cursive.

"You see, each letter melds into the next. Watch this." And together we created something out of nothing. "Steven R. Guttenberg—there it is."

There it was on the top of an A&S department store receipt: my name, looking like a Slinky going down a flight of stairs.

"There's your name, son."

It was so many years ago now. I watched in Arizona as my father walked his papers from the bedroom to the kitchen table, the mesh bag of his walker filled to the brim. He sat down, opened his checkbook, and took out his trusty Paper Mate. But after a few checks were sealed tight in the white envelopes, he sat there, frozen.

"What's wrong, Dad?"

"Can you fill in the amount here? I'm a little tired."

His hand was shaking.

I took the pen and finished writing the words "seventy-three" after his artistic script of "one hundred and." He looked at me with those sunken but focused eyes. I hated the fact that he got tired, more and more easily. The child I still was said that this just couldn't be.

Once I finally did get my driver's license, my dad celebrated me with my first car: a 1973 Chrysler New Yorker, my own piece of mobile real estate. The seats, the lights, the steering wheel: all mine. It was gigantic, and all my responsibility. I cleaned, washed, and waxed it for hours on that first day, my dad watching from the bay window of our house. When my mother finally strong-armed me into the house, long after it was dark, my father had the talk with me on my bed: about safety, about maturity, and, above all, about gas.

"Gas is very expensive," he said. "I'll pay for yours, but you have to only go to Russ. No ifs, ands, or buts."

This was 1975—gas was a precious commodity, more than we know now. There were true shortages back then, lines for days; you needed to know some tricks of the trade if you wanted to keep your tank filled up. Our trick was Russ down at the Esso station. He and my dad were friends; he did all the work on our cars. And I was being feathered in.

The Esso sign at Russ's became a beacon during the gas shortage. Russ carried a gun, the only man I knew, other than my dad, who had one. Russ wore his unconcealed in a holster, like an outlaw in an old Western. He had a busy mechanic's bay and took good care of those in his inner circle. He called my father early in the morning—four a.m.

"Come on down, and bring Steven. Meet me in front. We have gas."

My dad woke me from my heavy teenage slumber. I threw on my Converse and, still in flannel pajamas, we drove our separate cars through the snow, him leading the way to the long line that had formed at the Esso, even at that g-dforsaken hour.

Russ was at the pumps, gun drawn, watching everyone fill up: cars, gas cans, buckets, plastic bags. Yes, things had gotten so dire that people were filling up plastic bags with gas. He motioned for us to cut the line, and the cars that we jumped—at least the men—started to get angry, coming out of their cars to stand on the snow-covered pavement. Russ just pointed the gun at them until they got back into their cars, rolling their electric windows tight. Just like that, Russ beckoned us forward to the two waiting gas pumps.

My dad had real power. Neighborhood props.

As I fill up, I look around at the other cars at the Chiriaco gas station. I realize that I'm half-expecting to see the same family I saw at the rest stop after the pileup, all those people in a van. But they're not here.

There's a certain energy to a gas station like this—not the neighborhood filling pump, but one out on the highway, full of strangers going someplace else. Drifters. I look out at the crowd of unwashed freeway haulers, wondering how I look to them. I see families with little children, men in heavy work boots. A muscle car sits next to me: a Pontiac LeMans. Like the *French Connection.*

Out of the corner of my eye, I see a roughed-up man walking from car to car, his hands cupped, asking for money. I pull out some cash and hand it to him. If he can ask for money—if he can do that at a gas station—I can give him a twenty.

I screw the gas cap back in, return the hose to its holster, and rev up my Kia. I didn't fill it all the way—I'm playing the game, waiting to get out of California for those cheaper Arizona prices. The Gene Hackman monster next to me revs its engine and starts to pull out. The driver smiles as I let him get ahead of me. Disco blares from its speakers.

As I watch him go, I think about all the driving still ahead of me—and try to do what I can to keep exhaustion from creeping in around the edges.

I was shooting three to four films a year, flying between time zones, wrapping on a Wednesday night in Chicago and shooting another film Thursday morning in Austin. Something happens to you when you don't see a familiar and loving face for a while. There were times it felt like I didn't know who I was. I was flying so fast that I couldn't sit still, couldn't calm my heart. I couldn't grab hold of the moments. They were flying by.

That's how I was feeling when my dad called me that morning.

"Which *Police Academy* are you doing now?" he asked.

"Part three, Dad. Like *Richard III.*"

"Not quite, son. But the money's good. You can probably afford Richard's castle."

"Funny."

And then I was quiet for a little while. My dad asked me what was wrong.

"I'm here alone, Dad. There are lots of castmates, but it's weirdly lonely. I feel like I'm out in space. Like I have nothing to hold onto."

"I knew this would hit you one of these days. You've been going from movie set to movie set, without a real life. This is the time you pony up your emotional currency, Steve.

"I want you to try and sit still every day, grab a hold of twenty minutes. Close your eyes, sitting up, and just don't think of anything. It's called meditation in some circles. I just call it winding down. You need to get off the merry-go-round every day. You do, son."

I started to take time every day, just for me. I didn't know I was meditating. I was just sitting. But it was effective. I was able to slow my mind down. It soothed my nerves and gave me time to think.

"Do it every day, Steven, and I promise it will have an effect on you. A good one."

That was my dad. A man who could both describe a sophisticated electrical schematic and enjoy watching ballet. He loved rom-coms as much as action movies. He was a believer in the concept of yin and yang, and even had a world-class tattoo artist—Mike Rubendall—on standby to tattoo the black-and-white symbol on his behind. My mother put the kibosh on that one, but my dad had found other ways of expressing himself. Back when I was in high school, he'd even gotten an earring after a few drinks at a friend's party where a jeweler happened to have his piercing machine in the car. It made him look like a pirate.

The point was: this man loved new, different, next-level thinking.

And so, my dad followed meditation. He even carried a photo of Sai Baba in his wallet—my dad loved his values and his promise. My cousin Hughie was a devotee—he had a living arrangement in Shirdi Sai Heritage Village.

My father was a dichotomy, and that gave me such tremendous freedom to look for the next invention, the next idea, or the next promise without worrying.

Did my father take a few minutes every day at work to shut his eyes and croon, "*Ommm?*" I think he did.

There were times I looked at my dad and thought he looked not himself. I shrugged it off, not knowing his kidneys were compromised. (L to R) Me, Mom, Dad, and Emily.

My parents loved to come with me on some of my adventures, and when the studio sent a limo, it was all the more exciting. It meant we were going somewhere glamorous. There's nothing better in being famous than sharing it with those you love.

Chapter TEN

I see a blurry glow from the horizon—the sun is peeking out from the east. I watch as the eighteen-wheelers perform their dance: starting in their proper lanes, then leapfrogging over one another via the left lane, even though they're technically not allowed to be there. It's a game of polite bullying and patience. No one—and certainly not a pip-squeak in a Kia—is going to tell them what to do. It goes like that for a while, and then for a stretch everyone is in the proper place, and traffic returns to its regular flow.

I respect the trucks now—I understand the rules, how it all works. But when I first started making these drives, I got angry with them. I thought they were thoughtless, callous. They aren't, of course, for the most part; I know that now. So, I try and make sure to give the trucks plenty of space, no matter how badly I want to hit the gas and get to Arizona as quickly as I can.

I watch the sky turn orange. Daytime now.

We started doing dialysis four days a week instead of three. It was more work, but each individual session was a little more manageable—no more four-hour marathons of pulling blood. Saturdays were just about fluids—an easy two hours, no toxins.

Emily was coming out to Arizona with me more and more often. She helped bring my dad to the VA, and she gave me support and room to give time to my dad. It wasn't easy to watch my dad go through his arduous journey. She felt the pain he had, and she sat with him, holding his hand. Dad liked talking with her. It helped to have her giving kindness and love, and it elevated Dad to have Emily there.

I was getting my dad ready for one of his new Saturday sessions. I helped him from the kitchen table to the couch, where he wanted to rest for a little bit before getting dressed. Everything took more energy those days than it used to, and he'd gotten skilled at conserving it.

"Steven, look at this."

He gripped the skin on his arm. He was watching his skin wrinkle, and his legs get thinner. He pointed out the bald spot stretching down the back of his head.

"Am I going bald?" he said. He laughed and poked me.

"I think so, Dad."

"What?"

I yelled a little bit to make myself heard.

"You might be, Dad. But still handsome."

He grinned.

"Let's go get dressed. Put on some of the fancy clothes you got me from Europe."

He lifted himself up off the couch, but it was shaky going; I got nervous and handed him his walker. But he looked down at it and pushed it away.

"I don't need it," he insisted.

He looked down at his toes next, malformed into hammertoes from the army boots he trudged in for countless miles all those years ago. They were even more painful now, and sensitive to the touch.

"Look at my toes," he said. "What the hell happened?"

Everything had gotten smaller by then. His muscular back had shrunk; he was down to using minimal weights in the gym now. I thought about how much strength it must be taking him to keep going.

My mother watched him as he walked slowly back to the bedroom.

"Stanley, use your walker," she said, getting angry. "Use the walker!"

I handed it to him again, and this time he grudgingly grabbed hold of it. I'd watched my mother get sadder, angrier, and more afraid the deeper we'd gotten into dialysis. We all felt that way, though. Our lives had changed. She yelled at him; she was impatient and sometimes seemingly harsh. But I believed it was part of her desire to treat him normally. She loved him. At night, she watched over him from the other side of the bed while he slept and talked with himself. She listened to all that mumbling, staying up for hours and hoping to catch a sentence or two. I used to sneak down the hall whenever I stayed over in the house, trying to lighten the sound of my heavy feet, so I could peek through the crack of their door and check on them in the night. I watched them, fearful and worried and sad, hoping somehow to protect them.

It was still a surprise to me: how aging could sneak up on you and those you love—even those you don't know. The first time I saw photos of Robert Redford aging, it shocked me. How could that be "the Sundance Kid"? It was hard for my brain to accept—I only went there kicking and screaming. But there was no escaping it.

I was getting old too. The evidence was undeniable. Look at the shirtless photo of myself thirty-five years ago—I sure don't look like that now. What happened? Age happened, of course. Time. But I really thought I'd be that way forever. It wasn't just my dad. I was getting older too.

"Steve, pull up a chair and let us suck some of that youth out of you," Hume Cronyn said as he elbowed his wife, Jessica Tandy. She laughed loudly.

We were on the set of *Cocoon* in St. Petersburg, Florida. 1985. The air was warm and humid, but what I would remember most from that set was the wisdom and the laughter.

It was a beautiful day: bright sun, noon high. I was in my flip-flops and blue jungle-themed shorts. I spotted a group of elders giggling in the circle of directors' chairs and walked over to them, all muscles and hair. None of the *Cocoon* seniors are still with us today. But oh, were they alive in that circle.

Maureen Stapleton grabbed me by my bottom and guffawed. "If I could have an ass like that today, I'd give my eye's teeth."

I knew they were having a grand time with me, and I opened my can of Pringles.

"I'd like a couple of those chips, kid, and then bring me my proctologist because I won't have a normal poo for a year," Jack Gilford said, taking the can from me and giving it back.

Jessica sang: "Oh sweet bird of youth, bring me a flower."

Gwen Verdon laughed and grabbed a Pringle. "I'm not afraid of you, Virginia Woolf." She smacked her lips as she ate two.

"Enjoy your youth, Steve. It's such a damn fleeting mongrel," Don Ameche announced in his resonant and melodic voice, slapping my knee as he told me.

Wilford Brimley asked the group, "Hey, crusties, what's it like to get old? I have no idea. I'm a spring chicken!"

Hume and Jessica asked me out to dinner—naturally, I jumped at the chance. Jessica was the original Blanche from *A Streetcar Named Desire*, and a part of me still shook whenever she walked into the room. And I was going to have them both to myself for a whole meal!

We met each other in the lobby of the condos that Twentieth Century Fox provided and walked over to the neighborhood diner. These two superstars sitting in a booth, ordering burgers and fries with coleslaw, extra mayo, and coffee on the side? They looked like a king and queen, sitting with the common folk. But that was just the way I saw them—they certainly never acted that way. They were as comfortable in a Rolls as they were in the company van that took us to set every day.

"Steven," Hume began, "we brought you here to discuss a myriad of subjects, not the least of which is love."

He smiled as Jessica took his hand.

"Yes, Steven. Letters to your betrothed is ultimate in a romance, as is dedication and commitment. Pass the pepper, please."

I gave Jessica the shaker, which she generously applied to her cheeseburger.

"And focusing on your career can greatly help your relationship—purpose brings a human being much meaning," Hume said, grasping Jessica's hand even more firmly.

"But, Steve, we want to tell you, as an actor, one rule we've learned over the years. One important, unwavering rule. Can you guess what that is?"

Jessica's eyes danced as she nibbled on a french fry.

"Is it to know your character?" I blurted out. "His particulars, wants, and desires?"

Both of them shook their heads.

"Nope."

I tried again.

"Is it to find the meaning of the text, and how it relates?"

They took a bite of their cheeseburgers in tandem.

"Nope."

I was baffled.

"Is it to have the highest regard for your fellow players?"

They actually giggled at that one.

"Nope."

"Nothing about the characters, text, or co-actors? Then what is it?"

A pair of Cheshire-cat smiles appeared, and then both of them said, in unison, "Save your money!"

"That's it?"

They laughed.

"That's everything."

"At twenty," Hume said, "it's about the looks."

"At thirty," Jessica said, "it's about the cleverness."

"At forty," Hume whispered, "it's about the experience."

"And at fifty," they sang together, "it's about the cash!"

We had the most delightful dinner that night; I hung onto their advice like it meant the world. When I talked to my dad the next morning, he was impressed.

"Those two luminaries know their stuff!" he said. "Save your money, son—compound interest is a marvel."

"Dad, they said that too!"

"Of course they did! I sure would like to meet them someday."

My folks met Hume and Jessica at the premiere of *Cocoon* in New York; my dad talked with them about the stock market and CDs all night. At the end of the night, I watched as Jessica gave my dad a kiss on the cheek. He smiled bigger than I'd ever seen him smile before.

A few decades later, I was on the set of *The Goldbergs* playing Dr. Katman, the science teacher Adam Goldberg asked me to conjure up who's an enthusiastic mentor to Troy Gentile. There was a gaggle of young actors on the set, and now it was my turn to kid around with them. We were laughing about my prop work in the science lab. We sat in a circle of directors' chairs while I regaled them with my war stories of Hollywood, and they asked me for advice.

A charming young actress asked me, how does she get another agent?

Sean Giambrone, who played Adam, asked with excitement, "What classes should I take?"

A short and whispering kid with hair to his shoulders blurted out, "I loved you in *Police Academy*!'"

Then an earnest young man shouted, with a laugh, "I grew up on you!"

Hume and Jessica would have gotten a kick out of that.

My grandmother Kate was coming from Boro Park to stay with us. It was 1971, and I'd just had my Bar Mitzvah a few weeks earlier. My father and I were waiting for her at the train station with the necessities required any time we picked her up: a cup of coffee from the pizza shop and a pack of Virginia Slims, already opened, with a book of matches waiting.

The train pulled into the station, and the bar car men staggered out first. Behind them, in a puff of smoke, came a pair of high heels, a pink jogging suit, a bag of deli appetizers, and a travel bag: my gram.

"Hey, sad sack," she said to my father. "How you doin'?"

I saw my father fighting to keep his composure. He and his mother-in-law locked horns frequently—she thought that he should loosen up a little, especially with us kids. She knew my father's father, Grandpa Harry, a neighborhood tough who was known to pull men out of their cars and beat them up. Grandma Kate didn't like him, so much so that she had ripped my father's guest list to shreds ahead of his own wedding. When my father, noticing the absence of his large extended family at his wedding, asked her about it, Gram had said, "Oh, Stanley, I forgot to tell you. I ripped up the invitations to your family because your father is a cheap jerk."

Back at the station, she turned to me. "Hi, Tatie, light of my life. Want some gum? Stanley, the bags."

Back at the house, my grandmother unpacked the delicious delicatessen appetizers she'd brought with her: baked salmon, pickled herring, Nova lox, pickles, and bagels.

"Here, Stanley," she said as she laid out the spread, "a little of the old neighborhood to remind you where you came from."

"Katie, I'm Brooklyn, through and through. You know that."

"You'll see what I mean when you get older—when things hurt on your body a little more. You'll appreciate the old ways."

"I hope that never happens, Katie."

"You'll see. My doctor tells me I can't eat any of this crap. I have to eat a bland diet because of my stomach. But not this weekend, honey."

Almost sixty years later, my family sat around the table in Arizona eating dinner. Dad's plate was full of vegetables and chicken he hadn't touched. I saw him pointing to the rich, dairy-filled dish that my brother-in-law Bob was eating.

"Why can't I have that?" he said. "It's like I'm in prison."

"Dad, these foods on your plate will help you," my sister pleaded. "I'm sorry, but you have to be on this diet."

"I have to change everything? It's like I'm a kid, and you are the parents. No, I'm not going to do it. No."

I kept my mouth shut. It had been so hard on him. It hurts to tell your parent no, even when it's for their own good. The knife in my heart twisted a little deeper.

Every generation thinks the one before them is a bit rough around the edges. My parents didn't think Gram was up on the modern style of anything, and her edges weren't just rough—they were sharp as an X-Acto knife.

We kids always looked forward to going into the city to stay with Gram. She took us all over: the circus, the rodeo, Coney Island, and our favorite—dirty, filthy Forty-Second Street. This was before Disney took over, and it was the greatest. Bums, hookers, and three-card monte players lined the streets. Men sold hot purses and watches.

"Tatie, you want sunglasses?" she said to me. "Pick one out."

Time *to* Thank

The man had a selection of shades on a blanket laid out on the sidewalk, ready to fold up the moment law enforcement came along. I chose the aviators, the same ones my father had.

"Put them on, Tatie, let me see."

"There's no trying on, ma'am," the vendor said. "You either buy them or you don't."

My grandmother didn't take kindly to being ordered around by anyone.

"Shut your mouth, or I'll call a cop over, and you'll be in Rikers for a month. Go ahead, Tatie, try them on."

The vendor stood there, bewildered by this older Jewish lady with a Brooklyn truck driver's vocabulary, as I tried on the sunglasses. I stood on my tiptoes to look at the cracked mirror the man had on a hat stand. They were way too big for my seven-year-old face, but I still looked cool. Like my dad.

"You look sharp! Like a movie star."

"Like Dad?"

"I guess so. He is very good looking."

I gave her soft cheek a kiss, and she gave the man two dollars.

"If you didn't open your yap, I would've tipped you, but you acted like an ass in front of my grandchildren. C'mon, let's go get something for your sister."

And she held our hands as we zigzagged down Forty-Second Street, in search of a man she knew from Eighth Avenue with pocketbooks for sale. Gram was magic. She knew where all the best contraband was.

When we slept over at her apartment, the four of us—me, Gram, and my sisters Susan and Judi—shared her queen-sized bed. We watched *Chiller Theater* on the TV that sat on her dresser every Saturday night on channel nine—Gram loved gore. She lit up a Virginia Slim and then looked at us kids.

"Who wants to smoke?"

The three of us shot our hands into the air like we knew the right answer for a pop quiz. But this wasn't just smoking—it was a lesson in the art of tobacco, a tutorial in the regal grasp of the tobacco scepter.

"When you breathe in, just keep the smoke in your mouth and blow smoke rings, like this."

We each grabbed our own Virginia Slim and pulled in some smoke. Our rings were wobbly at first, but we became masters.

"That's it!" Gram said. "Now look tough and cool. That's it."

The four of us sat on the bed, smoking, watching TV, and jumping each time a monster loped across the screen. Around the middle of the second Creature Feature, Gram sent me to get a glass of water for her dentures. I was fascinated by that Brooklyn tap water: the way it poured out cloudy from the faucet but was clear by the time I brought it back into the bedroom. *Plop*, the teeth went into the glass.

"Gram," little Susan said, "can I try on your teeth?"

"Sure, SuSu, put them in."

Susan fished the teeth out of the glass, separated the top and bottom, and gingerly pushed them into her mouth. She weighed all of forty pounds and now had these enormous teeth in her head. Oh, did we all laugh. And then we all had to try the teeth on. The four of us giggling as we smoked in bed, wearing dentures and watching horror flicks on the TV. Now that was a party.

Dad was proud of the four troopships in which he crossed the Atlantic during the Korean War. This boat had much more luxury, and my parents loved it. I just wish I wasn't seasick most of the time!

A fashion show in Miami for fathers and sons. We had the delight of modeling Armani and Prada. Dad even got to keep his suit!

Chapter ELEVEN

Ticket number three was on a Monday morning. No one on the road except me and my lead foot. I opened the window to get a whiff of the early morning air and was hit with that sulfur blast—that unfathomable reek that hits me every time I drive into the state: welcome to Arizona. I sped past the sleepy lights welcoming me to the Grand Canyon State, feeling confident. My first two tickets were in California-land, and I believed the boys in blue were much less stringent across the border. Case in point: as soon as I cross that state line, the speed limit jumps up to seventy-five.

I was flying at ninety, my Kia humming, feeling good after its recent tune-up. I was good for a few hundred miles, I figured. Against the early morning dark, I could make out the dim outlines of cacti against the Sonoran Desert. The desert landscape out there feels like G-d designed it when they were awake. As opposed to the Mojave back in La-La Land, which feels like they threw together some sand and chaparral in a hurry when they were already late for dinner. My cell phone service blinked out, confirming what I could already feel: I was in the middle of nowhere.

The mountains greeted me as the road cut through the middle of a canyon. The road was mine; all three lanes were open for me to play with—except here came those two cherry red lights behind me. I wasn't alone, after all.

I pulled over as quickly as I could, hoping that I might get off easy as a reward for my obedience. I felt ashamed, though, of how cavalierly I'd been driving. And then I spotted it: an officer courtesy card, sitting in my console. I had collected, over the years, various cards from different police organizations, all of which held the alluring, implicit promise that perhaps one day they might get me out of a jam. There was the New Jersey state trooper provisional card, the New York Police Athletic League card, and the Keys to the Kingdom card. They had never worked before. But still, there it was again: hope.

The officer had a bright flashlight that flooded me with light in the pre-dawn dark, like a 10K light from a movie set. The officer was an older, no-nonsense guy, asking for all the usual stuff: license and registration. I kept my hands on the steering wheel, ten and two, on my absolute best behavior.

"May I take my hands off the wheel, officer, to open my glove compartment?"

He smiled. And I thought: maybe I have a chance.

"Of course, sir. And thank you."

He took my documents, and as I handed them to him, I noticed that his large and well-worn hand was missing a middle finger. I fought down the urge to ask about it as he made to head back to his cruiser.

"Oh," I said. "I have the courtesy card, from the New Jersey state troopers. May I give it to you?"

He grinned—what did that mean?

"Sure."

He came back ten minutes later and handed me the bad news.

"You were going ninety-four in a seventy-five. You look the same as in the movies, by the way."

Wait a minute—I was getting recognized.

"I know who you are. And I can't help you. I have to write this up."

So much for star power.

"You should have told me who you were. I wouldn't have charged you."

I didn't say anything, but I thought to myself, *Yeah, sure. That's always a good move. Announce who you are and expect special treatment from the state trooper.*

He handed me the courtesy card.

"And this trooper card? It's shit."

The cop waited for me to pull out. I accelerated to seventy and activated the cruise control. He passed me and didn't even wave. Somehow it seemed darker than it had been half an hour earlier.

I knew by then how close I was to having my license suspended. Four tickets, and it would be goodbye, license. The DMV was unforgiving, the judges unmoved when I argued my tickets, and the attorneys unhelpful when I called them. I was just one mistake away.

A Porsche whizzes by me as I think about that last ticket. I just don't like the guy. Where are the cops now?

But I have to watch myself. I become such a judgmental fool on these drives, left to my own thoughts. Driving every week isn't easy on me, but I can't admit that to myself. Instead, I focus on working the pedals and the wheel six hours straight. I don't use the cruise control as much as I should, and my body pays the price. I've been ignoring the signs, the constriction in my right leg that tells me to take a break. I finally got it checked out by an orthopedist a few weeks ago—the constant pressure creates stress on the muscle, causing it to protect itself in the form of ligament pain. He says there's a chance that I could have some sort of permanent damage that wouldn't be reversible. But I'll be okay. I'm not worried. Here I am, blaming my IT band for my discomfort, when really it's all me. You wouldn't work a machine without maintaining it properly, making sure it's oiled well. So why don't I stretch, do some yoga, take the breaks I need? Why do I treat myself like I'm invincible when I know I'm not?

Because I'm impatient. I just want to get there. That's it: I'll risk it all to get there. My dad needs me. I need him. I want as much time with him as I can get.

I watch as the Porsche weaves in and out of traffic, with no regard for anyone else on the road.

The first Porsche I ever saw was back in my early days in Hollywood.

My agent had invited me out to a very highfalutin restaurant—one of the most popular watering holes in the business. The food was Italian and the air heavy with the murmuring coming from the dark booths—men and women laughing, drinking, and trying to get one another's attention. The music was loud, and waiters in dark togs ran back and forth with flaming dishes. It didn't look like any Italian restaurant I'd ever been to before.

I parked a few blocks away—still avoiding the valet fees in those days—and was shown over to my agent's table. He was sitting with one of the most notorious producers in Hollywood. This man had had hit after hit for the past few years and was the toast of the town. But he was also known as a hooker-commandeering, drug-infested soul who could care less about human decency. All he cared about were the fireworks, the juice, the spoils of the game. I had only read about him before, and as I sat on the edge of the booth, I could feel the allure of danger in this man, like the gangsters I used to see in the Long Island diners.

He eyed me as I sat down for a moment, then continued talking with my agent as though I wasn't there. When I was finally introduced, he treated me like a side dish he hadn't ordered. I kept waiting for him to leave, so I could have dinner with my agent, and find out what was being cast and how I could get onto those projects. But my rep, too afraid to ask the producer to leave, instead accepted the waiter's suggestion of the lobster extraordinaire for the table. It was going to be the three of us.

This meant we both had to listen to Mr. Bigshot tell us about all his accomplishments and brag about all his clever seductions—of both unknowing young women and the business itself. I had nothing to say to him, nothing to contribute, so I sat like a bump on a log and waited for this guy to leave.

We ate the lobster—or, technically, *they* ate all the lobsters, and I filled up on bread. And throughout the night, famous faces—other producers, studio chiefs—came by to press his flesh. Anything for the possibility that he would grace them with his next project. But each time one of them came by to kiss his ring, the megalomaniac ridiculed them as soon as they'd left the table. My agent and I managed to exchange a few furtive glances, to confirm that we both knew what a character this guy was. Finally, once every sycophant in the restaurant had paid their respects, and our ears were cauliflower from all the talk, my agent paid the check and we got up to leave.

We approached the valet stand, and I said my goodbye and started to walk away.

"Kid," the producer said. "I've got a new Porsche. I'll drive you to your car."

I started to beg off—I said I *liked* to walk after dinner—but my agent grabbed my arm.

"He'd love to go with you," my agent said, winking at me. "He can walk later."

The man's souped-up exotica rolled to a stop, and as the valet got out of the car, I had a choice to make. I looked back at my agent, then to the producer, who was smoking a large cigar now and bobbing his head impatiently. I hesitated, and then I got in.

What made me do it? Ambition. That ugly monster that gives the hungry soul hope that by pleasing others, you'll get what you want. This man had the power to give me a part in one of his films. And all I had to do was keep him company for the block or two it'd take him to drive me to my Toyota.

I was lucky—the only thing he seemed to want stroked was his ego. Somehow he wanted to pontificate more than what he'd already vomited up to my agent at the table. And as he did, he pulled out a vial of cocaine. He revved the engine, shifted from first to second, and took a big snort off his index finger before offering the tube to me.

I had another choice to make. Accept it, go along with the ride, and make him feel like he was living right—or decline and probably blow any chance I had of working with him on a film. A split-second choice. Of course, whether I imbibed or not probably had nothing to do with getting work from the sleaze—he wasn't going to hire me. But like all working actors looking for a slot, I allowed myself to believe that by going along with the party, I might get a leg up.

But I said no.

"Not for me."

He shrugged, took another pop of the chemical snow, and stopped in front of my car.

"You gotta upgrade your ride, kid. It's junk."

I got out and watched his cartoon of a car drive down Melrose Avenue. I was proud of myself that I didn't do what I knew was wrong. No one gets a part by stroking a stoned ego.

It was another Wednesday—one of Dad's easier days. The sun was oven-hot in the Arizona summer sky. Emily, Dad, and I were heading over to the dialysis center. But as we left the house, I saw my dad wince when he noticed my car sitting in the driveway. The Kia was always my first choice when I was playing personal Uber for his dialysis run, but my dad felt differently.

"Let's take our car," he said. "Yours is not only filthy, but the bugs on the windshield disgust me."

I couldn't blame him. I'd driven in that morning and hit the inevitable large battalion of green-ooze-filled gnats that I manage to drive through every time, ten miles out from Joshua Tree. I can actually set my odometer by it—they're on time, every time, no exceptions. By that point in my long-distance commuting, I had actually started looking forward to seeing them. My bug friends. But no ordinary car wash could remove them, and it took a commercial grade window waxer to get rid of all the arms, wings, and leg fragments.

Plus, I liked the times my dad was blatant with me about what he thought. It reminded me that he was still, at his core, him. We walked towards his large, shiny Lexus.

"Now Steve, this is a car."

My dad showed his teeth when he said that. And inside, I was whooping with support for his pride. His walker slid easily into the oversized trunk.

My father was always a car guy. He treasured them. But with three kids, a cool sports car just wasn't in the cards.

All my father wanted was a new car. He saved up and finally made the purchase: a 1975 Ford Elite—two-doors, sleek and slick, chocolate brown with leather headrests. The night my parents picked it up, we celebrated like a war was finally over. We had a cool car; we had won. My father went to sleep that night dreaming of coming home the next evening, and him and my mother taking their victory ride up and down the Oyster Bay Expressway.

The next afternoon, I came home from school and put my greedy fourteen-year-old hands all over that brand-spanking-new chocolate delight. I opened the door—what substance, what heft! My sisters watched as I turned every knob, pushed every button. But once I closed the door, I heard a jiggle, a metallic shaking coming from somewhere. Clearly, something was off. And being the automotive expert that I was—after all, I'd ridden in *dozens* of cars before—I decided to check things out myself before my parents came home.

My sisters watched as I headed downstairs to the tool wall in the basement to select my equipment. A job like this, I decided, would require a Phillips head screwdriver and a sturdy set of pliers.

My sisters, once they saw what I was doing, implored me to stay away from the car. But I ignored them. They obviously didn't know I would be making the car better—fixing it before our folks came home from work. It was going to be easy. I just needed to unscrew the dashboard, find the problem, fix it, and then reattach the dash. And because I was also an engineering genius, it was going to be a snap.

Within the hour, I had the dashboard of my parents' brand-new car in pieces. I looked and looked, but I couldn't find the loose nut or bolt or whatever metal doohickey that was the problem. I decided to end the search and reattach the dashboard. It would be as easy as taking it off, I figured.

But—and this was a big but—the thing just wouldn't line up. The darn dashboard was having issues getting back to the way it had been.

"Ford," I thought to myself, shaking my head. "What's wrong with that company?"

My sisters stood there, shrugging their shoulders.

"They sell us a car, and the dashboard doesn't fit exactly where it started after I pull it off its hinges? When I'm old enough, I'm going to write them and complain!"

By now, the whole dashboard was askew. The steering wheel was at an odd angle, the air vents stuck on closed, and the radio knobs looked like notes on a staff of sheet music in an ascending arpeggio. Not exactly what my parents had seen that morning, when they'd sat together in the car before heading into work. It had ten miles on it.

My mother came home from work first. I was in the den with my eyes on the driveway and my two sisters on the floor watching TV. My mother got out of the old Dodge Dart, still wearing her whites from her assistant job at Dr. Dribbon's podiatry office. She slid her finger along the candy caramel lacquer that glazed the car from grille to trunk. She opened the screen door to the house, practically sighing with contentment.

"Kids, is that not the prettiest car you've ever seen?"

I sat there, frozen. I'm so screwed, I thought to myself. But my sisters actually managed to keep my foolery to themselves. I was safe—but only for a little while.

Then I heard the van pull up. My dad jumped out of the van like it was his birthday. He laughed while looking at the car, full of a deep, visceral delight. This was my dad's trophy, the sign that he had made it. Then I heard a muffled voice coming from outside.

"Hey, the car is unlocked. Who was in here? Steven?"

I slinked away from the den and out to the car. My sisters followed, keeping enough distance so they'd have time to get out of the way in case my father hurled my body across the lawn. By the time I got to him, my dad was sitting in the passenger's seat, the door open.

"Steven, the dashboard of the car. Do you know anything about this?"

He was calm—that was his trademark. But my sisters were on the brink of a nervous breakdown. They knew something my dad didn't, and that was too much for them. Both of them started to sing like birds.

"Daddy, Steven had your screwdriver..." Judi said.

"Stop," he said. "I want him to tell me."

Dad wasn't even using my name. I was "him."

It started with, "I kinda..." and then for ten minutes straight I pontificated about why the car wasn't up to snuff, how the dashboard was a lemon because it wouldn't line up again correctly, and how offended I was that Ford wouldn't take the hypothetical letter that I'd never actually gotten around to writing seriously.

My father started to grind his teeth. My sisters were squirming behind me, awaiting the punishment. But all my father asked was that I go upstairs; he said he would be up in a little bit. I could sense my sisters' disappointment as I walked back into the house—there went all their hopes for a little afternoon entertainment.

I walked up those two flights of stairs like a prisoner on his way back to the hole. I heard from downstairs the sound of my mother's voice.

"What did he do?"

I stood at my window, looking down at the chocolate Elite, still pristine except for my foolishness. After a time, my father appeared in the doorway. He sighed and sat down on the bed.

"Steven, what were you thinking?"

"I thought I could fix it."

He looked down at the colorful shag rug beneath his feet.

"Sit here next to me."

My father had spanked me before. He even gave me the belt every once in a while. But that day, all he told me was that it was a new car, there was nothing wrong with it, and that touching, taking apart new things, especially cars, was a bad idea. Mostly he just sighed a lot.

"I love you, Steven," he said. "But I don't know what the hell is wrong with you."

My mother and father still took their ride that night, the dashboard at a seventy-degree twist. They drove up to the North Shore, to be among the fancy houses, the smooth roads, and the quaint little shops. And every time they stopped—to get candies at the old-fashioned sweet shop or to see the bay inlet where my dad could majestically park the car next to the water—there was the dashboard, askew.

About a month after the dashboard debacle, our house on Wyoming Avenue was graced with another mechanized miracle: a brand-spanking-new dishwasher. This had been my mother's dream: after so many years of handwashing every dish, pot, and pan in the kitchen, here was a machine to wash and dry them on its own! The stinging cuts and rashes would be a thing of memory.

"Be home after school for the dishwasher delivery," my mother told me that morning. "Just tell them where it goes, under the old cabinet your father took out, and give them this ten-dollar bill. Then don't touch it."

That afternoon, with my sisters watching and my parents once again at work, I let the workmen in. They came in with this enormous brown cardboard box, looking like they were carrying the Ark of the Covenant. They looked authentic enough in their matching uniforms. But once they got to work, they sure seemed confused about finding the hot and cold pipes. Didn't they do this all the time? Shouldn't they know how to find the right water pipes the second they came into the kitchen? That was my first clue that these guys didn't know what they were doing.

I watched as they installed the only thing my mother had ever wanted (other than a kid who behaved). After they left, I cleaned up the kitchen and stood before the new machine, staring at it. Lots of buttons. Had they hooked it up correctly?

Those buttons—they were an addiction. I couldn't help myself. I had to run my fingers over the set of five: *start, rinse cycle, sanitizing, fast wash, heat dry*. What did they mean? Did they really run this thing? One touch of a button, and it started.

My mother had given me *explicit* instructions. But I decided to override her request. I just had to press two buttons. If one was a good wash, then two had to be great.

"Steven," my sisters said, "Mommy is going to kill you."

They might be right. But if I had died every time my mother said she was going to kill me, I would have died a thousand deaths by then. So, I pushed the two buttons.

They did not snap back into place. Something was wrong.

It had to be the machine and the guys who installed it. I shouldn't have given them that ten-dollar bill, with such shoddy work. I decided to fix the problem myself. And, you got it, I was going to unscrew the front panel—the dashboard of the dishwasher, if you will.

Down to the basement I went, my sisters' wails of disapproval echoing through the house. Even the dog put his paws over his eyes. I grabbed my old friends, the Phillips screwdriver and the pliers, and ran back up to the kitchen. I unscrewed the back of the washer door, revealing the inside—the brains of the machine. I went looking for the buttons, skillfully navigating through the tangle of wires to get there, and pushed them back into place. But, lo and behold, when I went back to the front of the dangblammit machine, they wouldn't work. In fact, when I put the door back together, screwing in almost all the screws that had been sitting on the floor (*what were these two extra screws for?*), the dishwasher wouldn't even start.

I sweated out the next few hours. It wasn't pretty. My mother walked in and had a shit fit. Again, my father filled the doorway of my bedroom, and he wasn't as gracious an executioner as he had been with the car. He left my room with both of us feeling lousy, and this time I was the one who asked the question.

"What the hell is wrong with me?"

My mother washed the dishes by hand that night, staring at the brand-new dishwasher loafing in the cabinet as she scrubbed pots and pans. My father just shook his head—this had been an expensive mistake. And I was numb, still asking myself the question that seemed to be on everyone's lips.

Still, life went on after my bungles. I sulked, my sisters played in the living room, and my parents watched TV. Eventually, we all went to bed. I lay under my covers, staring at the ceiling. And after a while, my dad came in.

"Just want you to know that I believe in you. Even with these two screw-ups. Good night."

That was who my father was.

Mom, Dad, and me in St. Mark's Square in Venice. I stand behind them, as they have always led the way for me. If only I could remember all the lessons they taught me.

A big deal for my mom and dad. Dad especially
was moved that our surname was getting hon-
ored, and his son who delivered newspapers on
that road now has a street named after him.

Chapter TWELVE

O nce I've settled in, the drive feels like second nature to me. The mountains and patches of sand along the highway in Arizona become familiar. I look at my watch; I'm making good time.

There's an old, abandoned building on the north side of the 10; I watch it as I go past, feeling its aura. There's no one around—not a soul. Nearby is a weary gas station, void of life; a weed-covered garden; and a parking lot saddled with garbage. This building used to be a restaurant, thrumming with hungry travelers. Most of its windows are broken now, but inside are the original tables, the counter, the ancient kitchen equipment.

Someone built this place. Craftsmen spent time on the cornices and the wooden plank floors. The rooms are now worn down by the rain and wind. There is some dignity left, but few visitors. I stopped there once, months ago, to wander the spaces. I watched the way the walls leaned in the sun, the floors covered with leaves and debris. I imagined how the lonely side windows once revealed the crowds sitting inside. Like seniors left behind and families long gone, this place was deserted. As I walked through, the echoes of my own steps felt paltry in comparison to the liveliness that must once have been here. I feel for this building, inanimate but still alive, clinging to what it once had. Like it wants me to know that it, too, had value.

As I left, I found myself touching its walls, petting it like an old dog.

The sun is getting higher in the sky; I see my reflection in the polished chrome of the gas tanker in front of me. I move to pass it. The open road is ahead of me now, and I squint and put my visor down against the new morning light. There's a photo of my dad clipped to the visor. He has those dark aviators on and a white tank top, his muscles roaring.

We were at a meeting with my dad's nephrologist, Dr. Robey. And Dad couldn't wait to tell her all about his workout routine.

"So I'm in the shower, doing push-ups. I can do dozens of them!"

Dad demonstrated with his hands from his chair. Dr. Robey looked down her glasses at me.

"And in the gym, I'm using twenty-pound barbells. Much lighter than I used to use, but they still give me a pump."

Dr. Robey looked at my dad, and then at me again.

"This is very hard for me to tell you, Stanley," she said, pausing for a breath. "I want you to stop working out with weights."

"What?"

My father was stopped cold in his rush to tell his story. His mouth hung open, as did mine.

"Do you really have to do that?" I said. I was fighting for his right to do what makes him, him. "It's his love. His hobby. His everything."

"Since I was twelve years old, I've worked out with weights, Doctor," he said. "I've kept in shape. My triple bypass grew new veins because of my exercise. And now, I can't?"

Dr. Robey looked down and gathered herself.

"How's about just doing exercise with no weights?" she said. "Just body weight?"

He looked at her with those coal black eyes, blinking in disbelief.

"Dad, should we order?"

"In a minute," he said. It was later that week, and he had enough energy to go out to lunch. He had pulled out his softly worn wallet to bring out several faded photographs of my grandmother Sadie. He loved lore about his childhood, especially Army tales and stories about his mother, a talented designer at a local Brooklyn millinery. He liked to talk about how she was from Austria but spoke English so well that she became an interpreter and letter writer for the whole Jewish neighborhood. The pictures he proudly showed the waiters and waitresses were of her in the stylish hats she designed. "I have a story I want to tell."

He talked about his father, who Grandma Katie had disliked so strongly she disinvited his extended family from his own son's wedding. My grandfather was physically strong and simple in his wants, a man who exercised his body before it was fashionable and became an accomplished power lifter.

"My father's friend, Mr. York, was a forefather of the exercise craze. He created York Barbells. You ever hear of them?"

Our young waitress, Erika, couldn't have been more than twenty-three. She shook her head no.

"I didn't get along with my father," my dad said. "But I adored without limitation my mother. And throughout my childhood, I vowed to be a good father to my future kids."

He put his hand on mine.

He told Erika he was a moving man by trade, one of the many sons of The Guttenberg Moving and Storage Company that his grandfather Jacob started. Jacob would do feats of strength beneath the Brooklyn Bridge: lifting people, weights, and even horses.

"And as the *pièce de résistance*, he would lift a Shetland pony three feet off the ground. Did you hear me? I said three feet!"

Dad laughed a little.

"So, a black-market chiropractor friend suggested to him, 'Jacob, you are so strong. Take your wagon to the harbor with your horse, and move people from Ellis Island to their new homes.' My grandfather took that advice, and by hook or by crook—mostly crooks—built a major trucking company, with their headquarters at South First and Hooper and Williamsburg, Brooklyn."

"Erika," I chimed in. "If you have something to do…"

"No, I'm loving his stories."

My dad elbowed me and grinned. I stood back and let him run, delighting in the moment. It was like he forgot about his life with dialysis and the chair, tubes, and the techs running around. He was cute and charming, and his hearing aids let him not hear what he didn't want to hear—one of the few perks of being hard of hearing. He loved women, especially when they complimented him—he ate up their praise with a spoon. He needed this now, more than ever: a brief return to what had been normal in his life for so long.

Finally he ordered, and we ate.

"You see, Steven?" he said. "People love my stories."

When I was eight years old, there was no better day than a Saturday. Because on Saturdays, Dad took me in to work with him.

My father's work took him a long way from the moving company days, a long way from his days as a New York cop too. By the mid-sixties, he had found his calling, working for different electronics companies. And we—his family—were reaping the benefits.

He was working for an electronics company called Adelphi. They had a store out front for retail electronics. Every Saturday, my dad went into the office early, around seven a.m. He'd open up and do paperwork in his office until the Saturday crew came in around mid-morning. The Saturday crew mostly worked in the warehouse, led by a man named Gordon whom my dad liked to call Flash. But the real stars were the guys who ran the retail store: all of them young and cool and hip, with the latest clothes, the latest slang, and the latest moves. And every Saturday at lunch, we would go—all of us, me and the big guys—to a bar-restaurant to have meatball heroes. It was the greatest feeling an eight-year-old could have, sitting there with fifteen adults trading stories and jokes, the dirtier the better. I was mesmerized, and I could tell my dad loved to see me soak in all that testosterone.

I waited all week for Saturday—for my meatball hero and a table of cool guys. The only thing that made those Saturdays even better was when my dad took me, once a month, to go get my hair cut.

The barber my dad went to was right across the street from Grumman, the aerospace company. They built military equipment, planes, and tanks. They also built the lunar module, the one that would someday go to the moon. The moon! Grumman was a big deal, and so was this barber shop, with man after man waiting to be cleaned up. They did it city-style: the hot towel on your face and the massage machine on your back. The shop was crowded with businessmen, lawyers, and all sorts of stylish people. The room was filled with cigar smoke, the music of Cousin Brucie on WABC, and the hum of men talking: sports, cars, and money. These were friendly, clubby guys, and my dad and I were part of it, there amid the smell of Barbasol, Hai Karate, and Old Spice.

My dad waved to his barber. Richie was a hip guy, and I didn't know until years later that he actually wore a toupee—I just thought he had the coolest pompadour, black and shiny, like Elvis with scissors. He finished up on a big blond guy and motioned us over, and I felt like I belonged. Richie shook my hand and showed me to the most comfortable chair on the planet. My dad held up a finger in acknowledgement—*you're one of the guys*. Nothing topped it. Dad got a shave after Richie was done with me, and we walked out of that shop looking like two million bucks.

"Hey," my dad said, "I have a friend who works at Grumman. He's there today—want to go see him?"

Grumman? The secret fortress across the street, surrounded by guards and electrified fences, where the astronauts were? Grumman even had a replica of the lunar module on the roof. There was entrance after entrance with military personnel at every gate. Important people going in and out, like something out of a James Bond movie. And there we were, at the gate, Dad asking a guard about a guy he'd met at the office.

We were let in and directed to the main building, the two of us looking sharp in our new haircuts, smelling good, feeling good. Dad saluted every soldier we came across—it was like they knew he was a soldier too, a Ranger, a hero. A guard took us through a labyrinth—room after room, people inside in gas masks and white gloves, measuring things with mysterious machines that emitted puffs of steam. Every two seconds, the view of the labs made my skinny body jump with excitement.

The guard pressed a button on the side of two large doors, and my dad's friend Chaz came out, covered head to toe in white.

"Glad you took me up on the invitation!" Chaz said. "Come on in. Who's this?"

My dad introduced me.

"Short for Charles, young man," he said. "Nice haircut."

He led us up to an observation room, through another set of plastic-coated doors and a curtained window. There were other people there, but I was the only kid.

"You men can sit here, I need to get back to the LM," Chaz said. "Hey—no one gets to see this. No one."

He put out his hand, and I shook it. He had "NASA" embroidered on his white one-piece. NASA! The curtains on the windows opened, automatically like we were in a movie theater, and there it was: the lunar module itself, surrounded by a dozen people dressed in science-fiction white.

My father put his arm around me.

"There it is, Steven. It's going to space—to the moon. And you get to see it. Cool, huh?"

Chaz waved to us as I sat there, spellbound. It was a funny-looking thing: legs that seemed like they were from a charcoal barbeque, and what looked like aluminum foil on its head—like the kind my mom wrapped chicken in. Lots of antennae sprouting off its sides, steam coming from somewhere, and scientists fawning over it and brushing it with tiny, feathered tools. It was history. I could feel it.

And my dad gave that to me. He didn't smile too often, but he smiled at me then. He held me close and kissed my forehead.

"It means so much to me that we shared this together."

I was in the last three weeks of filming the movie *Short Circuit*, and my father—trained as an electrical engineer—loved hearing about the details. He had always had the feeling that if enough electricity could be generated, and if Ohm's Law was true—meaning the current through a conductor between two points was directly proportional to the voltage between two points—then life could be created. Assuming that those two points, in this case, were a heart and a brain. I know it sounds far-fetched, but a pacemaker gives the heart an electrical current, and it's what Mary Shelley proposed would bring her monster to life in *Frankenstein*. So the idea that a robot—a pile of steel bolts and aluminum—could feel and act like a person, with real human emotions, fascinated my dad. He was on the cutting edge of the semiconductor world and thought the thesis of *Short Circuit* was a real possibility.

The director, John Badham, had come to fame with movies like *Saturday Night Fever* and *War Games*. He and my dad chatted on the phone a few times about the notion that this robot called Number Five could actually have real emotions and thoughts. They agreed that it wasn't likely in 1986, but that sometime in the future these computer-generated beings could mimic, and even authentically experience, certain organic moments. And isn't that kind of what AI is all about today?

We were about to shoot a scene where I tell Number Five a joke—the idea was that this would be the true test of the robot's ability to have human intelligence. My dad called me up in Astoria, Oregon, where we were filming, and I told him that I needed a joke to tell the robot.

"Steven, tell them the rabbi, minister, and priest joke—the one with the circle."

"Isn't it too dicey to bring religion into the movie?"

"But that's exactly what this movie is about. It's about giving life to someone, and that's the responsibility of G-d. And G-d is religion, isn't he or she?"

I was still a little skeptical, but my dad had a point. I asked him to tell me the joke again, and I listened intently.

"Dad," I said afterwards. "Isn't that a little stereotypical?"

"Don't be so precious. It's funny! Ask Mr. Badham."

I was sure that anything controversial would be dismissed by the producers, but I decided to give it a go anyway. The set was bustling with a hundred crew members the day of my big scene. John Badham was sitting in his director's chair, and the puppeteers were rehearsing the robot's intricate moves. There were seven skilled artists handling Number Five, and they all had to work in unison to make it look like the machine had really come to life. I asked John if I could run the joke by him first.

"No," he said. "I want it spontaneous—let's do it on the first take. It'd better be good, Steve."

It was a master shot, which meant both Number Five and I were on the screen. So I had to get the joke right, with enough intention and timing that it was truly funny. Everyone on set—the lighting crew making changes in the middle of the scene, the camera assistant geared up and twirling the film inside the Panavision, and the puppeteers at the ready—had to actually think the joke was funny.

John yelled, "Action!" and I started my bit.

"There's a priest, a minister, and a rabbi. And they have a pile of money and are deciding how much to give to charity. The priest says, 'Let's draw a circle on the ground, and throw the money in the air; whatever lands in the circle, we give to charity.' The minister says, 'No, let's draw a circle on the ground, and throw the money in the air, and whatever lands outside the circle, we give to charity.' And then the rabbi says, 'No, no, no. We'll draw a circle on the ground, throw the money way up in the air, and whatever G-d wants, he keeps!'"

There was silence. The robot turned his head one way, then another. I looked at the puppeteers. I could see Badham out of the corner of my eye. And there was nothing. The joke fell flat.

Or so I thought.

Then there was an explosion of laughter. The robot was hysterical; John and the crew were cracking up, the puppeteers doing their best to stay in character. And I swear, Number Five came to life. He was moving in ways I had never seen in other parts of the movie: he was giggling, he was grinning, and his face took on a brightness that was unique to that moment.

It worked. My dad's joke worked.

After the scene, I sat down at the lunch table with Tim Blaney, the main puppeteer and voice artist behind Number Five. He looked like he'd seen a ghost.

"Steve, when you told that joke, I was ready to react, my hands on the controls. But something happened. Something weird."

"What do you mean?"

"It was as if Number Five came alive. Like he really thought it was funny. My hands moved, I'm telling you, in mysterious ways. Don't tell anyone, but for that moment, he was alive. Your electrical energy, maybe. But he was alive."

I couldn't wait to tell my dad the next morning.

"Really?" he said on our daily call. "Isn't that incredible?"

"Dad, I'm telling you. I looked at that robot, and he was alive."

"One day, Steven, the scientists will create a way for computers to think on their own. You just watch."

And my dad was right. Now computers can laugh and feel and create moments like that with artificial intelligence. I'm sure there's going to be more to come too. "Just you watch."

A Thursday morning—one of my dad's days off—and my sister and I were making him breakfast: a hard-boiled egg, cream of wheat, and the vegan grilled cheese if he wanted it. The Boost sat near the measuring cup so that we could monitor his fluids intake.

It was a little after seven, and Dad still wasn't up—that was weird. I walked lightly down the hall, being careful not to wake them up if they were still sleeping. I cracked the door. Dad was sitting on the bed, rubbing his head. His dark eyes looked smaller than usual. He squinted as the light from the hall reflected off his striped pajamas.

"I don't know what the hell is wrong with me."

I put my arms around him.

"There's nothing wrong with you, Dad. Nothing."

I directed my dad in a film, and for the only time in my life, he had to do what I said. Alas it only lasted two months—the length of the shoot.

My dad in the 82nd Airborne, with his compadres in front of the truck they called the "Angry 46." It was this truck that saved his life as he slept under it while a tank company came silently through, crushing all his friends in their sleeping bags.

Chapter THIRTEEN

My steering wheel starts to shake. The Kia probably needs another alignment, I figure. I check the other indicators on the dash, just to be safe. The temperature gauge looks fine. The fuel gauge… Wait, I'm on red. How could I have not seen this before? It's due: the bill for the game I like to play of waiting to fill up at a cheaper station. It's on empty. This can't be happening, I think. I look at how many miles I have left: one. One mile? How is that possible?

The car starts to shake and heave. Is this what an empty tank feels like? The car sputters, and the automatic steering goes limp before stiffening up. The car pulls itself to the right, almost automatically. The verdict is in. I gambled like a fool, and I lost. I look at my watch; it's nine thirty.

I decide to call AAA. But my phone has no bars, zero, no reception this far out into the desert. I try for it anyway, but there's no signal to dial the number. Someone, I figure, has to come by eventually.

I'm stopped now by a brick building I've noticed before on the drive. It's a pile of ancient bricks about two hundred yards off the pavement, with no roof. I've never seen it up close before. It looks smaller from here than it did from the road, whizzing by on my way to my dad.

I've got stories, it seems to say.

There is no one on the road going in either direction. The wind blows, and a dirt devil kicks up close to the far side of the brick building. It picks up momentum, like it's daring me to chase it. There's a hawk sitting on a rotting fencepost—all these details I could never notice from the car. But none of them changes the fact that I'm still out of gas.

Not knowing what else to do, I make my way over to the brick building. The sand is surprisingly deep as I tread through it. The wind, the dirt devil, and the hawk are all making a little noise, but otherwise it's quiet, and I'm alone. This is not good.

I cautiously approach the building, thinking that all I need is for one of these walls to come down and pin me. At first glance, it looks empty. But as with the restaurant I passed earlier, the closer I look, the more I can see remnants of a life lived here: a table and two chairs, dust outlines where pictures hung, a hairbrush on the floor. No garbage here; remnants instead of a real family life. The roof is wide open, and sunlight floods the space. I dare to sit in one of the chairs; it's oddly comfortable. The hawk circles above me now before swooping down and perching majestically on the side of one of the walls. It's watching me, and I'm hoping it's not going to come down and scratch my eyes out. It couldn't do that—could it? The dirt devil keeps chasing its tail about a hundred yards from the front wall, and the wind is dancing on the floor at my feet, moving that hairbrush oh so gently. I close my eyes to take it all in.

"Who are you?"

My eyes snap open. Standing in the doorway is the largest state trooper that Arizona could possibly grow. Next to him is a German shepherd almost as big as he is.

"Get up slowly," he says, his hand unsnapping his holster. "You're trespassing, buddy."

"I'm out of gas," I say. "I just wanted to see this place."

This isn't how it's going to end for me, is it?

"This is private property. The old adobe is owned by the Cocopah Tribe, and it's protected by the state. Get up slowly."

He seriously thinks I might try something. I look up and the hawk is still there, its wings spread.

"Walk out of the building, please."

I do, slowly, and stand in the sand. Still not another car for miles except mine and the cruiser. I notice that he's older than me, and weathered as that old fencepost.

"Hands behind your head."

"Really?"

"Really, shithead."

I put my hands up, and he handcuffs me. I notice that he, too, is missing a middle finger. What is it with state troopers and middle fingers?

"Over to your car," he says. "I'm retiring next week. I need this like a hole in the head."

We go to my Kia.

"You don't mind if I look around, do you?"

"Uh, no?" I say. I sure hope I don't have an old joint hiding somewhere.

"Lucky, watch this guy."

The giant shepherd sidles up next to me and starts panting. Oh, man.

The trooper is very thorough in his search. He's deep in the back seat when he calls out, "What's this?" and pulls out the knife I carry with me. He comes forward and stands towering over me. I can feel his breath.

"It's a knife," I say. I can feel the sweat dripping down my back. The dog stops panting and looks at the trooper.

"You have a permit for this?"

"Do I need one?"

"You're going to need a lawyer. You're going to jail."

"No. You can't do that. It's just for protection—I would never use it. Please. I have to get to my father in Peoria."

"Yeah, yeah. Let's go."

He leads me to his cruiser and opens the back door. My phone rings.

My phone rings? There was no service here.

"Can I get that, please?"

"No, you cannot. But I can."

The hawk starts to fly in circles above us. The dirt devil comes so close that I can hear it.

The trooper grabs my phone from the console of the Kia. His large finger presses the answer button, and he puts the phone to his ear.

"Hello? No, it's not."

A beat.

"I'm State Trooper John McGillicuddy."

Another beat.

"Your son? He's trespassing on private property, sir. I'm about to read him his rights."

A long beat.

"Really? Where?"

He listens, looking at me now through dark aviators.

"My family is from Bushwick."

Another beat.

"That's my grandfather's name."

He listens for a while.

"The Seventeenth? Are you kidding me?"

He takes his glasses off and sits on my passenger seat. The dog lies down.

"Mr. Guttenberg, that's my grandfather. I was named after him. I haven't heard his name for a long time."

He pulls out a white handkerchief and wipes his face.

"I rode in that car, sir. I remember his laugh."

He's quiet for a long time.

"Can you tell me, sir. What was he like on the job?"

I watch as he and my father talk. My father was regaling this man with stories of walking the beat with his grandfather, nearly seventy years earlier.

"He liked that free food, didn't he?" the trooper says with a laugh, leaning on his knee. "Can I get your number, sir? I'd give anything to hear more."

They talk for a bit, the number jotted down in his ticket book. And then he hangs up and comes over to me, shaking his head.

"This has to be G-d or something. Your dad worked with my grandfather, in the city."

I just looked at him.

"Really?"

He walked behind me and undid the cuffs.

"Sorry about that. Your dad did a good job. He was on the job when it was really hard. He must be a strong man."

"He is. And still soft inside."

"Me too, buster. You're free to go. Be careful out there—it's a weird stretch of highway."

He walks over to his cruiser, and I get into the Kia, sweating like crazy. Then I remember.

"Hey!" I call out. "Can you give me a ride? I'm out of gas!"

"I can do you one better," the trooper says. "I've got ten gallons in the back—I'll fill you up."

He pulls out a mammoth can of gas from the trunk of his cruiser and does just that. And as I pull out, he stands there with his dog, the dirt devil still spinning behind him and the hawk sitting on top of the brick wall. He and the dog are smiling, and his four-fingered hand waves goodbye.

All the dumb courtesy cards I've collected over the years don't mean a hill of beans compared to my father's words. Once I'm back on the road, I give him a call.

"Dad," I say. "What did you tell that cop?"

"Never mind what I told him. You're driving, aren't you?"

"I am."

"Then get here! I've got a birthday to celebrate."

He's all business today. And he sounds good. I haven't heard him sound this good in a while.

I had bought my dad a new walker. The Drive Nitro—the Ferrari of walkers, compared with the Chevy Blazer he'd been using. Now, he had an indoor walker and an outdoor walker. I brought it home from the store, took it out of the hatchback of my Kia, and gave it a spin myself in the driveway before bringing it inside.

"What do you think of this?" I said.

"Another walker?"

It was clear that I was much more excited about it than he was.

"But you can get around. You can walk. You can move. You have independence."

He shrugged and gave it a try. I could see that he had lost some more weight; it bothered me. He stood hunched, his eyes looking hollower than I remembered, darting back and forth, with dark circles. The days when his eyes shone gave me a lift. Those days weren't coming all that often anymore. But when he looked at me, I lifted my eyebrows—it hid my frown. I had become talented at disguising my melancholy.

Mondays were the hardest days. The toxins had built up over the weekend. This one was particularly bad, and I found myself whispering to my dad as he sat in his oversized chair.

"I promise you—we'll get you home. You can get in bed and relax. Your breathing will come back."

But it didn't. He was having such a hard time getting his breath that I took him home early from dialysis and laid him down to get some rest. He just couldn't get enough air. I stood there, lost and unable to help him, wishing there was some way to put my own breath into him and let his lungs fill on their own. Slowly he managed to catch a little air, and gradually returned to himself. But it was clear that something was wrong.

"Dad," I said. "We need to see someone."

We drove to a lovely doctor in Sun City—but isn't every city in Arizona a sun city? He prescribed my dad oxygen. He was concerned about the fluid in my dad's lungs and hoped the dialysis would extricate it.

"You mean one of those tubes in my nose? All day?"

"All day."

Both of us walked out of that meeting with our heads hung low. Oxygen, twenty-four hours a day? Another new way of being. We bought two machines—whenever my father walked to the middle of the house, he changed breathing tubes, like a scuba diver doing rescue breaths. A portable oxygen exchange came with us every time we traveled out of the house. We all had to carry oximeters now to make sure his O2 levels stayed above ninety. Everywhere he went, the plastic tubing announced to the world that the man needed extra wind in his sails. It sucked.

I started to notice the changes in the other people I saw regularly when bringing Dad to dialysis. Barbara, who we saw that first day, had gotten weaker, unable to get out of her own wheelchair and sit down. The techs had a hoist—they'd strap Barbara in, lift her up, and swing her over to her chair like a crane sweeping a concrete pipe across a construction site. I saw the way Barbara watched all the eyes in the room on her, so we looked down to try and give her a little privacy. But I could see the way the straps strained under her, pulling on her fragile skin before she was deposited into her chair. No one came to dialysis with Barbara; she was alone for the whole session until a young woman—a niece, or a granddaughter—came to pick her up at the end. I always tried to ask Barbara how she was doing when we passed her in the lobby. Sometimes she just shrugged. Sometimes she asked me to pray for her. Some days, she didn't show up for her appointment. I would breathe a sigh of relief when I saw her again.

Dave—the ordained minister with a chemical company who loved McDonald's—sometimes didn't come in for his appointments either. Not good. But when he was there, he liked to tell me stories, letting me know who he was outside his kidney failure. He built his own company, looking after leaks in oil reserves and natural gas storage stations. He spent most of his time traveling, on the road to provide for his wife and children. He was honest and funny when he talked to me, the port in his chest visible as we spoke.

Eddie was a beefy Latin man who stopped by to check in every session; he finished his dialysis a little before Dad. He was friendly and generous and made sure to thank my dad for his service, pointing to his Korean Veteran hat. He and I started to talk too—he called me "Brother," held my hand, and wore his religious beliefs proudly on his sleeve in a way that gave me a warm feeling. He had lost his wife a few years earlier, loved his kids, and was close with his brother. But no one was staying with him; he drove himself to the clinic in his Camaro muscle car. He told me in a soft voice that he was having other health issues; it might be cancer, he said. He needed to get more tests.

It started to feel like the paramedics were coming in every other session. Someone would get sick and need more attention than the RNs could provide. It was tough, seeing the fire department EMTs roll someone else out of the clinic. The rest of the herd watching as one of their own was taken. Some of them we didn't see again.

And then there was Brad. The young rock star of the clinic, the one who could hook himself up to the dialysis machines. I was fascinated by him and how different he was from everyone else. He was so laid back, wearing his signature pajamas. I wanted to know everything about him.

Some days, his mother came in with him. Eventually she came over and introduced herself to us. She was a nice lady, and I had to ask, "How does a young man like Brad deal with this?"

She looked at me with kind eyes.

"Brad has not worked since he started dialysis. That's ten years. He's thirty. He lives in an apartment with a cat and a roommate who is a fire lookout. During fire season—which is longer now with climate change—he gets sent by the forest departments to possible fire zones. So now Brad lives alone for six months of the year and has the place to himself."

"And what does he do with his time?"

"I think he does the best he can."

I drove my dad home in silence after dialysis. He started to moan a bit to soothe himself. The ride home on days like that needed to be short and sweet—no conversation, nothing that would drain his energy any further. I knew to be careful about putting the seat belt across his fistula. I made sure there were some Dum-Dums lollypops for him—the gourmet ones I used to buy took too long for him to get through, and Dad just loved the Dum-Dums. Music helped, sometimes. I put on "Earth Angel" by the Penguins. It was his favorite and had become one of mine too.

Susan and I took turns bringing Dad to his sessions. But after the hospital, seeing him get worse, I found myself coming in even on my off days. She would drop him off around ten, and then I'd sit with him for a few hours, so she had time to run a few errands. I bought a new chair to sit on for the sessions—the stools they had weren't doing any good for the ligaments in my legs. I had initially asked if I could bring a wooden one in from the waiting area—they'd been taped off anyway, in deference to Covid protocols—but the RN had given me a curt no. So, I bought my own chair. It helped a little, but the tendons in my right leg still felt strained. I didn't dare get an MRI. I didn't want to know.

Dad was particularly cold that day when I went in to take my shift. Susan had left him with the hood of his sweatshirt up, and he was bent over like a homeless man I used to know in Santa Monica. I took his blanket and tucked it tightly around him, trying to trap in whatever was left of his body heat and hopefully make things a little more comfortable. But I don't know if it was helping, or just something I did to make myself feel better.

Susan came back to relieve me. On the drive back to the house, she called me.

"Steven, there's blood everywhere near his fistula. You didn't see it?"

I hadn't noticed anything. Neither had the techs, and they were supposed to look at the fistula when they came to check the machine every twenty minutes. I waited for them to come back home.

Susan was in no mood to talk. I sat there feeling terrible. There was nothing I could do but try and be more vigilant.

I was in New York, staying at the Carlyle Hotel on the last leg of the publicity tour for *The Bedroom Window*, a Hitchcockian thriller directed by the great Curtis Hanson. I'd been looking forward to going to New York the entire tour, because my folks were going to come into the city and enjoy some of the spoils of the movie star life with me.

I was set up in a two-bedroom suite on the eighteenth floor: three thousand square feet of luxury, rare antiques all around me, and a spectacular view of the city. My parents met me a few hours after I settled in. The Carlyle was famous for two things: it was the hotel where Kennedy had his affair with Marilyn Monroe, and it had the Café Carlyle, where Bobby Short held musical court. And that night, Bobby Short serenaded my mom with one of her favorite Johnny Mathis hits while my father sipped Dom Pérignon.

I was sitting back, taking it all in, when my publicist came into the café. She tapped me on the shoulder and told me she had some news, but that we should go into the hallway to talk.

"This is not what you want to hear," she said, "but there is a death threat on your life. And the message is that he's going to do it at the David Letterman show tomorrow night."

I was supposed to go on Letterman to do my bit to promote the movie. But what did this threat mean for all of that? My mind was spinning. But then I felt another tap on my shoulder. It was Dad, who had followed me out into the hallway.

"I'll take it from here," he said.

The publicist stammered an offer of help and asked who she should talk to.

"No one yet," my dad said, ushering me back into the café. We finished the evening without another mention of the death threat.

I didn't get much sleep that night. By the time I got out of bed, my dad already had an update. He'd been working the phones: his old precinct, the Seventeenth; the Letterman Show security; and a few connected people in town. Dad didn't have many friends, but he knew a lot of people. They might not have talked for thirty years, but when he put up the Bat Signal, they returned his calls.

He explained to me that death threats are usually a hoax. But this one was particularly strange, because it was supposed to happen while I was being interviewed.

"The only action we can take, Steven, is vigilance. The cops will be there, trained eyes. I'll be standing in the back. It'll be like how El Al does it—all of us will be watching for certain triggers. Other than that, you'll have a vest on. And if you get hit, it'll deflect the metal."

"Get hit?" I said. "As in get shot? Are you kidding?"

"Yes and no, Steven. I don't think it's going to happen. But I do want you to wear a flak jacket."

My stomach was in knots the whole rest of the day. We wandered around Central Park with an NYPD officer alongside us. Was it all a hoax, or was someone really going to try to kill me?

We went back to the suite to dress for the show. My publicist spent most of her time in the powder room—she wasn't taking the stress well. My mother tried three different outfits on before deciding on a dark pantsuit. Hopefully not chosen to hide the blood, I thought. My blood!

Down in the lobby, my father met up with two undercover cops. We all drove over to the Ed Sullivan Theater and emerged to find a large and vocal crowd, all screaming my name, wanting an autograph, a photo. "Not today," my father said as he ushered us past the crowd and in through the backstage doors.

By this point I was used to doing the talk show circuit to promote a new movie: I could feel the usual anticipation of being on the couch, trying to be a great guest and tell my stories. But I knew, as I felt my father's hand on my shoulders, that this was going to be different. Either there was someone in the audience who hated me enough to try and murder me, or it was a hoax that had cost me and my family, friends, and colleagues all this worry for nothing.

There were more cops backstage than I had ever seen at a talk show. As we walked to my dressing room, I could tell the staff was more somber than usual. They all stared at me a little too long as I passed. Inside the dressing room, my mom stared at me too, but then flashed a quick smile.

"Remember to duck, kid," she said.

The producer, Bobby Morton, came in to tell me I'd be the first guest. We went over the stories that I'd given to the segment producer, and then he brought up "the thing." That's what he called it, "the thing." My father reminded me about all the undercover cops in the audience, the cops in the halls, the eyes in the lobby. They were doing everything they could to make sure I was safe.

I heard Paul Shaffer start playing his music and listened as Letterman did his monologue. A page came back into the dressing room and said it was time. Was it just my imagination, or did she say it the same way I'd heard them call for a man who was on his way to the electric chair?

My mother laughed.

"Steven, I'm sure they're a bad shot. Just move serpentine, like in the movie *The In-Laws*."

"Not funny, Mom!"

She smiled and raised her glass of soda.

"Oh, don't be silly, Steven. Nothing's going to happen. I hope!"

My dad pulled me aside.

"No matter what," he said, "don't mention the threat."

Letterman announced me, the curtain opened wide, and I walked out onto the stage, scanning the audience. I kept imagining someone—a madman with wild hair and a sweaty face—standing up and yelling, "I hated *Cocoon*. Now you die for that, Guttenberg!"

But there was nothing but an enthusiastic audience and Letterman smiling wide with his hand outreached. He knew—I could tell the way he gave my hand an extra squeeze on the handshake. I knew, and he knew, and it was the only thing on my mind. I saw my dad in the front row, next to an undercover cop. He put his finger to his lips as though to remind me: no mention of "the thing."

I sat down, and Letterman asked me how I was. I blurted out, "Fine, Dave, except for this death threat 'thing.'"

My dad threw his hands up in the air. Letterman shoved past my comment to his next question, trying to ask me about the movie. But the audience was abuzz. "Death threat?" They just couldn't settle down. I talked as fast as I could, describing the narrative of the movie, the location of the shoot, and how great it had been to work with Isabelle Huppert and Elizabeth McGovern. But I just couldn't keep my eyes off the crowd. Where was this person? Was it going to happen?

But there was nothing. And then the commercial break came. I chatted with David and Bobby Morton. I saw cops crisscrossing the crowd in quick movements, like blue ants swarming over a picnic blanket.

Then came the second segment of the interview. Then, a handshake with David.

"You survived," he said. "Good one, Guttenberg."

I walked off the stage and felt my dad's large hand on my shoulder.

"I gave you one instruction, and you did the opposite. And I know why."

I asked him to tell me.

"Because, Steven, you thought it would scare the perp into not acting. And, second, you like a good show."

"Maybe, Dad. Or was I just not in control of my wits?"

"You are always in control. You just choose to go the other way sometimes. Learn a lesson. Fish with closed mouths don't get caught."

We drove back to the hotel, my father eyeballing the entrance to the Carlyle. We got out of the limo. A man ran up to me with his hand inside his suit pocket. I didn't notice it at first, but a plainclothes came out of nowhere and rushed at the man. But before the cop could hit him, the man pulled out a *Police Academy* Mahoney doll and a Magic Marker.

"Mr. Guttenberg, could you sign this? I'm a collector. And a fan."

The cop looked at my dad, and my dad gave him a nod. I signed the action figure as my mom got out of the limo.

"You guys were afraid of a little doll?" she said. "Gimme a break!"

My dad wore his uniform every military holiday,
still svelte, fitting his US official like a glove. He
did have it tailored, though, while he was in the
service, always having an eye for sleek lines.

The whole family on Christmas Eve in Pacific Palisades, California. Dad would get on a plane and arrive ready to have a good time. He treasured moments and would say often, "That's what creates a life, Steven. Moments."

Chapter FOURTEEN

There's an apple on the floor of the passenger seat, rolling back and forth. I want it. I think about pulling over, but there's no need for that. I unhook my seat belt, keep my left hand on the wheel, and check behind the Kia. No one in any direction for miles. I stretch down with my right hand to grab the elusive fruit, groping around blindly against the floor mat. For just a couple of seconds, I cheat my eyes away from the road.

The car swerves way onto the shoulder. I pull myself up and crank the steering wheel back the other way—the car swerves across the highway, fast, and it takes me a few more moments before I have the thing under control again. It felt for a second like I was going to tip over. I look around—still no one. There's a smell of burning rubber in the air, and an apple in my hand. Dumb move. The apple isn't worth it.

A little while later, I see a Love's gas station up ahead, sitting lonely in the middle of the Sonoran. I decide to stop and fill up, top it off. Nozzle into gas tank, credit card into slot, pick the octane, and let my car gulp. A man in a wheelchair-accessible van pulls up. I can see the portable oxygen concentrator on the side of his wheelchair as he hooks up the van and rolls into the convenience store. I can feel the wind on my back, the desert sands drifting all around me.

It had been a bad day at dialysis. His blood pressure soared, his heart rate climbed towards one hundred, and he shook beneath his blankets—more than just the cold of the room, his tired body was fighting a fever, an infection. I had to carry him from the clinic doorway to the Kia. His breathing got even more shallow once we were home, and my sister quickly determined we had to bring him to the doctor. It was the first time in a year they needed to bring him a wheelchair for the doctor's office, and after an excruciating chest X-ray, the doctor sternly advised that we bring him to the ER.

I slowly walked out to my car as Dad carefully navigated with his Drive Nitro walker. I made sure he didn't bang his head as he slid into the passenger's seat.

"Keep breathing," I said as I gently pulled the seat belt across his thin frame. "Please, Dad."

"I'm trying. Please don't take me to the hospital."

But I had to. The only other option was calling 911, and I knew my dad would hate that, the ambulance showing up and strangers taking him for a ride. We drove in silence until we got to the Mayo Clinic. He looked at me with wide eyes and a sigh as we pulled up to the ER.

"Why are we here?"

An orderly approached the car.

"Because you can't breathe, Dad."

But he wasn't hearing it. He wouldn't get out of the car. The orderly and I looked at one another, and I tried again.

"It's just a little checkup, Dad," I said. "That's all."

The orderly nodded in agreement, trying to gently coax my father from the car. It was terrible, treating my dad like this, lying to get him into the hospital. But it worked. We got him in the wheelchair and brought him into the ER lobby, where they ushered him into a triage room and took his vitals.

"Please don't let them admit me," he said.

The Mayo Clinic is a great organization, as far as hospitals go. But my father didn't want to spend the night in any hospital, even a good one. They brought him from triage to a patient cubicle with sheets hanging on all sides, and that was where the stress and worry started to really seep in. Nurse after nurse, doctor after doctor. An IV into his hand, just in case, and multiple diodes to monitor his blood pressure and heart rate. My father was still wearing his Korean Veteran hat; he got thanks from everyone who scuttled briefly through those sheets to his bed. The woman on our left complained about her bladder. The man to the right was in pain, screaming for relief.

My dad looked at me and then rolled his eyes. This wasn't where he wanted to be. He looked up into the ceiling, as though searching for an escape hatch. Any way to get out of here.

A doctor came into our small holding pen and introduced himself.

"Mr. Guttenberg, first of all, thank you for your service."

My father tipped his hat—his old-school charm and respect still shining through, despite everything else.

"Yeah, what's going on with me?"

"You want to get right to it, huh?"

"I want to go home."

"We're trying to figure out why you are short of breath. And I don't think we can do it here. I want to admit you."

The doctor put his hand on my dad's, the one with the IV sticking out of it.

"No," my dad said to me. "I don't want to be admitted. I want to go home."

My sister came into the room.

"Dad, it's probably just for some tests."

"I could give two you-know-whats. Just let me go home."

That was how my father felt about staying in a hotel room built for machines that plugged into his body, to be woken up every four hours by strangers intent on poking and prodding, taking your vitals without knowing your name. Sue and I sat there, wallowing in our father's disappointment, the pain of it heavy on our already splinter-ed hearts.

Hours later, we walked behind as his bed was wheeled through hallways, crowbarred into elevators, and finally deposited at his designated suite at Hotel Mayo. My father looked at all the new faces, nodding along to the instructions.

"What else can I do?" he said, looking at us with eyes as black as onyx.

The pulmonologist was going to visit tomorrow morning. As in four a.m. Sue looked at her watch—it was only seven thirty p.m.

"I'll be staying the night, if that's okay," I said. The head nurse nodded.

"We don't do this for everybody, but I'll make an exception."

I told Sue to go home to check on Mom and look after her husband and daughter. The nurses rolled over a reclining chair for me that reminded me of the first-class seats on American—or the chairs in the dialysis clinic. They gave me sheets, a blanket, and a pillow that had starch dripping from its case. But after a few good squeezes, it was as soft as a puppy. I pulled the chair over to Dad's bed, and we watched reruns of *Seinfeld*.

I must have fallen asleep, because the next thing I knew a nurse was waking me with a nudge, my dad still holding my hand.

"I didn't want to wake you," he said. "But they are taking my temperature."

My father smiled as I rustled awake and pulled my chair over to the front of the bed. It was eleven p.m., and as soon as the doctors had come, they were gone again. I pulled up the blanket, kicked off my sneakers, and tried to settle in for some sleep. But the subtle blinking lights and constant beeping of the oxygen counter kept me up. I covered some of the lights with towels, trying to muffle the beeps. Whenever the oxygen fell below ninety-two, an alarm sounded. And the only way to shut it up was to get my father breathing more.

"Breathe, Dad!" I yelled, trying to make myself understood through his hearing aids. "Breathe through your nose. We need to get the oxygen up!"

I hated yelling at my dad. It was shameful. I tried to keep cool, but sometimes the yells came out as emotional outbursts. I just wanted him breathing. Walking. Running. Lifting. Back to being the dad who told me what to do, not the other way around. It was painful, and I could feel the pain expanding, growing to fill all the hours of my days. Sometimes I closed my eyes and thought about everything my father was going through: being stuck, getting blood drawn, urine samples. All of it awful.

I had noticed my own body changing too. It felt selfish to think about, but I couldn't help it. I wasn't eating regularly or with any focus on nutrition. I wasn't going to the gym.

At four a.m., the nurses came in for another check. I put my sneakers on and stood up. Everything looked okay. The pulmonologist came in afterwards and loaded my father's oxygen canister up with medicine. I asked him what he thought. He looked down before he told me that my dad was going to keep needing oxygen twenty-four hours a day.

This was not the first time we'd heard this news. But each time hurt more, and confirmed that things were getting worse, not better. My father was reading the pulmonologist's lips, and he shoved his head back against the pillows when he made out what the doctor was saying.

I nodded off briefly and woke up again an hour later to watch my dad's breath on this machine that would now be a constant companion for who knows how long. His breaths had a tremor at the end of them as the oxygen pushed into his nose, making an effort to rescue his lungs. Another hour went by, and then there was a flurry of new nurses, coming to check him out. Finally, a bit of good news: Dad could go home today.

Sue came into the room with a smile; she knew that all we needed to do was sign some paperwork, and then we could take Dad home. A nurse provided pen and papers, Sue signed, and a wheelchair arrived. My father eyed the portable oxygen machine uncomfortably. He had been hoping to be off the juice, and now he just had confirmation that he needed it more than ever.

"This is just terrible," he said.

"But it helps you breathe, Dad."

"Yeah, yeah."

As I walked behind Sue, my heart fell to the linoleum tiles. Dad never wanted this.

We drove my father's Lexus home, the portable breather lurking in the back seat next to Sue. The breathing tube made its serpentine way around the seat to my father's shirt, entering his nose. It had been recommended to him that he stop driving, and that bothered him immensely. He could still drive—I knew he could—and I was the only family member pushing for his independence behind the wheel. Being able to go to the dry cleaners and the gas station was a sign of his sovereignty, his liberty, his power.

"For Chrissake, I just want to go get Dunkin' Donuts. You're taking that away from me?"

The ways we were trimming away what it meant to live as an adult were disturbing to me, and I couldn't imagine what it did to him deep down. We were taking away the last things he could do for himself.

How could this happen to someone who had been so strong and capable?

It was a Tuesday, November 9, 1965. We were still living in the two-bedroom apartment in Flushing. After school, I went over to Sam Toron's house—he was a giraffe of a kid, who seemed to be able to touch the top leaves of the maple trees in front of his family's apartment building. He kept all his toys on a top shelf, completely out of my reach. It was getting late, the sun dipping beneath the antennae on the rooftops, and I was begging him to pull down the Gumby, when an emergency bulletin came across channel nine from the TV set in the living room.

"Con Edison has announced a disaster at their main station. All electricity in the tristate area will be interrupted indefinitely. Please prepare…for a blackout."

My desire for Gumby and his loyal horse Pokey was abandoned as Sam and I ran to the TV. The screen was now ominously playing images that reminded me of the time I had stayed up late enough to watch the station give its goodnight. Sam's mother screamed for us to close the windows and search the apartment for anything we could light on fire.

"Wood, matches, toys, flashlights, candles. We can tie socks to sticks for torches if we need it. It's a blackout, kids—no heat, no television, no electricity."

What? No electricity? I had images of the end of civilization as I had known it: gangs of thieves roving the streets in scary masks, the prison gates disarmed, and scar-faced convicts set loose on Flushing. Sam stood there while his mother and I commandeered every piece of flammable material in the apartment. We were without a man. Sam's father was delivering seltzer—I was sure his truck would be rendered useless. Soon, I thought, cars would pile up on the George Washington Bridge, and people would be fleeing their homes to run through the streets with the gangs and the escaped convicts, leaving us law-abiding citizens to their mercy.

I was all alone—except for Sam, still frozen before the TV; his sister, who kept playing with her dolls like she didn't even know the world was ending; and his mother, who by now had piled mismatched rags, sticks, and flashlights next to the television. And then it was dark. I thought of Passover, Pharoah threatening the Hebrews with destruction and paying for it with the plagues. What was next, locusts? We couldn't even see in front of our hands. This was a blackout, all right. The radio, which Sam's mother plugged in, stopped mid-sentence. Our only hope of communication was the transistor radio, which had batteries from the 1940s.

"I'll kill Irving—he has no idea how to make sure we have emergency provisions."

There was something oddly comforting in hearing this—did every mother threaten to kill their husbands? Mine certainly did. But the comfort was short-lived.

Sam came out of his stunned spell and fell to the shag carpet, crying uncontrollably as we tried to find him in the darkness. He was writhing on the floor, and it took his mother a minute before she could grab him and start slapping him to try and get him to stop.

"Stop it, you baby. Get a hold of yourself!"

Slap slap slap. Like something out of a movie.

Outside the window was a complete and utter absence of light. The green and red neon light of the Camel Filters sign had been extinguished. The cowboy on the competing Marlboro sign, who usually rode up and down on his horse, now stood motionless, staring at the sky like he was hoping to ride off onto the range. The only light came from the handful of apartment windows that had the faint flicker of candlelight. But the sound amid that blackness was a roar: people screaming for their loved ones and cars meandering through the streets, piled up at the intersections with no traffic lights to guide them.

The world was a catastrophe, we had no emergency provisions, and I started to really get scared. I thought about my family: What would they do for food? How would they survive? Would I ever see them again? I imagined my mother, trapped in the frozen food aisle of the A&P, the peas, carrots, and string bean packets melting and the water flooding the aisles. My poor mother, navigating the shopping cart with my sister in it, fighting with the other mothers to stay afloat and grabbing the economy-sized cereal boxes as makeshift life rafts. Was my father stuck in a subway, the electrical impulses going wild underground? How would he climb his way out of the hundreds of feet of rubble, the metal train cars twisted beyond recognition? I imagined the shards of glass and spikes of metal as he fought to escape the hellhole that Con Ed had caused by losing their grip on the ohms that controlled the whole tristate area.

I stood at the window contemplating my fate as Sam's mother held her children in the darkness, cursing her husband for his lack of preparedness. I strained against the darkness to watch the confusion in the streets, hearing other children's cries, looking down at people stumbling to and fro in the street. But there was one stalwart figure marching down Kissena Boulevard—a steady torch of light coming from his hand, his wide shoulders in a leather jacket—striding purposefully towards the white brick of the Torons' apartment building. He looked up to our window, positioned the flashlight under his chin, and smiled. It was my father, his face lit ghoulishly by the flashlight, giving me a salute.

"Steven!" he called up. "I'll be up in no time. Stay put."

"But there's no elevator!" I said. We were up on the twelfth floor.

"That's nothing—a mere walk in the park. You tell Betty I'll be right up. I brought provisions for her."

I turned around, and Sam's mom had lit a match, her hand shaking as she tried to light the candlewick on top of the lifeless Sylvania.

"I can't light this thing," she said. "Hold the candle, Sam."

But he was no use—his hands were shaking.

A knock came on the door. Betty opened it, and a beam of white light flooded the apartment. My dad grabbed the matchbook and, with one hand, lit the candle. He had a bag of batteries, a transistor radio, and an ice chest filled with milk and eggs. But more important than any of the individual items was the powerful sense he carried with him: everything was going to be alright.

"Betty, I'll stay until Irving gets here."

And then Sam's mom fainted into his arms.

He laid her down on the plastic-covered Castro convertible and started setting up the battery-operated camping flashlights he'd brought along with him. Sam, Sam's sister, and I beamed at him so wide, it was like the electricity in our three faces could have powered all of the tristate area, or at least Queens. Eventually Irving made it home, and Betty lambasted him for a little while before she gave in and fell crying into his arms. All was well. She didn't actually kill Irving.

My father carried me home on his shoulders, giving me a safe bird's-eye view of the streets of Flushing. There was plenty of confusion, but none of the marauding gangs I had imagined, and no striped convicts stealing purses and breaking windows.

After a little while, my dad turned his head and said, "Want to walk with me?"

I climbed down from his shoulders and held his thick, smooth-skinned hand all the way home.

Our two windows were the only ones lit up in our entire apartment building. My mother leaned out the windowsill when she saw us coming; she was smiling.

"You got him?"

"I do."

"It's me, Mom!"

"Come on up—I've got supper."

My dad had been prepared. We had plenty. We sat around the brightly lit kitchen table, my mom and dad laughing together, my little sister holding her doll. No one was crying—actually, it was fun. In fact, it was one of the greatest nights of my life. My dad was surrounded by the light of his flashlights and the glow of his family. He grabbed my hand, and he winked.

"See? It's okay, son."

I got a call from Rob Thomas. I'd worked with him a few years earlier, doing an eight-show run as a villain on *Veronica Mars*. This time, he wanted to talk to me about *Party Down*. The show was a sophisticated comedy about the staff of a catering company out in Hollywood. The story he pitched me: Steve Guttenberg has a birthday party at his mansion. The people from the catering company show up to his house, but nobody's there. I pull up in my Porsche and tell them it's the wrong day. The staff is deflated, but "The Gute" says, "Let's party anyway! Just you guys and me."

What ensues from that premise is a very funny episode about a compassionate-yet-lost-in-movie-stardom guy—me!—and the pragmatic and ambitious guys and ladies of the catering company, some of them aspiring actors and writers hoping for their big break.

The "Steve Guttenberg" I'd be playing in this episode was an eccentric, extravagant free spirit who delighted in having these strangers in his house. And as I read through the script, I could tell that the fictional Steve was very uninhibited. In one scene, I would join Lizzy Caplan and Adam Scott's characters in "my" hot tub, *sans* bathing suit. I had a few other scenes with my shirt off. Thanks to my dad, the gym rat, I knew how to train hard for the month before I would be on camera. I've done it for many movies with my shirt off: *Cocoon*, *Police Academy*, *Three Men and a Baby*. So, when I knew I had a month, I dieted, ran, and worked out like a few hundred thousand people were going to see it. And when I did the show, I was ready.

Being a guest actor is like being the new kid in school. But you're only there for a week. So you have to earn your place, your position. Sure, you come in, and there's some celebration of your accomplishments. But after five minutes, your whole resume is pushed to the side, and what's called upon instead are your skill and your talent. Then I get to work.

I felt especially excited about this job. It was a very smooth-running, hot show. The cast members were getting great press. Rob and his producing group were stellar—they knew everything about a twelve-hour-or-less day, and how to get the pages completed. I even had the luxury of visiting the production offices to meet with the producers and some of the actors ahead of shooting. There are times when actors don't want to meet you before you work, but this atmosphere invited it—it was the right thing to do. I met Adam Scott, a delightful and aware person; Lizzy Caplan, who I found to be such a smart lady; Ken Marino, such a funny and decisive actor and writer—he really has a gift; Ryan Hanson, a Jimmy Stewart kind of guy, charming as all get-out; Martin Starr, with whom I created a friendship; Megan Mullally, one of the most elegant and theatrically intelligent artists I've ever met; and Christopher Mintz-Plasse, so smooth, consistent, and unflappable.

The shoot was one of those great experiences where you show up for work and everyone brings their friendly and sharp A game. What a great relief it was to be around capable and talented filmmakers! We were shooting at an enormous home, filled with all the extravagances you'd expect from an over-the-top Hollywood personality. Since it was a big house, we could shoot room to room, getting scenes done while prepping the next room. And digital filmmaking meant fewer lights were needed, making the pace even quicker. We shot quickly, and with such precision. And I have to say, I think you get better performances from the actors that way. The waiting around is cut down to a quarter, and you get a kind of momentum, not only for the actors, but also the crew—a flow.

My character was meant to be completely trusting, funny, a rascal—and I got to have a ball throughout the entire episode. Ken Marino and I did a scene where he was touching "Steve's" aquarium—only to discover that the tank is an art piece, filled with a piece of ice from a glacier that costs $10,000. Now *that* would definitely be the taste of a fictional Steve Guttenberg. Ken is a smart and funny storyteller. When I get to work with guys as talented as Ken, I just follow their lead, knowing it's going to be a good scene. And that's how it went. Ken cracked me up—he knew just how to play being embarrassed when he got caught with his hand in "my" aquarium. I also got to do a few scenes with Megan Mullally. She's just top of the list. Her talent and ability make you know you're sitting with the best. If you know Megan's work, you know she is a master of acting.

When it came time to shoot the hot tub scene, I was grateful to my dad all over again for those nights in the weight room growing up. Adam and Lizzy's characters were shocked as I slipped in, thinking nothing of it, like I was having my body massaged by the water. It was just such a fun and easy scene, and an intelligent approach to what could have been a bit crude. Rob and his writers knew the rhythm of the show so well, and the scene did its job. The last scene had me stealing Ryan's date with my shirt open. Totally gratuitous. And hilarious.

The real thing that struck me was how good everyone was. The crew and cast kept me on my game. Everyone threw friendly fastballs—they're nice, but they work hard and fast, and you have to keep up. I'm usually a bit nervous before I work. I know my job, but I'm ready for the unexpected: changes in dialogue, scenes, anything. And *Party Down* kept me on my toes.

Time *to* Thank

The real pride of this show is having people come up to me to tell me how great my episode was and that it could be the funniest of the show. I see it as funny, but knowing the quality of the talent—both in front of the camera and behind it—I find it hard to believe my episode rises above the rest. But I'll take it. Sometimes, the work is just good. That was this show.

Dad and my wife Emily. They would chat about her hometown, Buffalo, life and its journey, his military years, and his career in electronics. They could chat for hours, sitting by a fountain, looking out over the Kelly green golf course.

Dad and I at an HBO shoot when he started to have issues with his kidneys. He had to come to the set; he dressed up and wanted to see his son work.

Chapter FIFTEEN

There comes a point in every drive when it seems like the road will never end. I try to fight the feeling as long as I can. I'm deep into the Arizona desert now. I think about my father in a party hat. His eighty-ninth birthday—how many times has he told people about it? He repeats things these days. He used to make fun of my grandmother for repeating certain instructions. And now it's how he moves through the world. I don't like the reminders that they are getting on in years. He repeats more than ever now. I have no right to be irritated by it. But I am. It makes me feel selfish.

There's that judgement that comes to me when I've been trapped in the Kia with nothing but my thoughts for so many hours. I save the loudest judgments for myself. But time is a-wasting, and the only antidote for judgement is getting to where I've been traveling to all this time. I press on the gas and accelerate, trying not to think about cops or how close I've gotten to losing my license.

I already had three tickets, and I was getting pulled over again. I looked down at my speedometer as soon as I saw the flashing lights: ninety-two miles an hour. The highway patrol walked up fast from the cruiser over to my window.

"What the hell are you doing?" he said. "It's seventy-five here, and you blew past me like a tornado! License and registration."

I sat in a panic. I knew what would happen with ticket number four. Goodbye, license. Goodbye, I-10. Goodbye to this life I had built for myself since my dad started dialysis. And this trooper was serious. I didn't even have time to do any old-fashioned begging before he had my information and was heading back to his car.

It was ten long minutes before he returned. Ten minutes to think about the stupid risk I'd taken, wanting to get to Phoenix a few minutes earlier. To think about kicking myself for not being careful when I knew I couldn't afford another ticket. To think about all the mistakes I've made—and there have been a lot of them.

He came over to the car and leaned in.

"I'm not going to write you up," he said. "You're my wife's favorite actor. You get a bye week. Have a good day, Mahoney."

And with a tip of his hat, he went back to his car. *Police Academy* had saved me. What a lucky break.

My sister heard a whisper from our favorite tattooed tech, Wendy. It was a hush-hush option—not many knew about it, and even fewer could obtain it. Private dialysis. Professional training to become a certified dialysis technician. Dialysis at home. The real thing.

We had changed dialysis centers, driving out to Sun City four times a week for my father. It felt worth the longer drive, at first: less crowded and a little more attractive in a superficial kind of way. We still waited for the chair, but that was how this worked. Then things changed. It got busier. The patients' physical maladies were more acute. We started seeing more mistakes, and the industrial machines were harder on Dad's system.

Susan started to weave together a basket of contacts. These were people who knew when and where there was training to gain that instruction, both artful and scientific, to administer the elixir. It would give life, extend life, sustain life—at home. And that was the key word: home.

After a few months, Susan got another whisper from our favorite tech. She'd heard that there was an opening—and Susan should jump on it. And jump she did.

No one was more excited about the prospect of at-home dialysis than my dad. He started talking about it at every meal. Imagine: waking up, brushing his teeth, and walking into the den to be hooked up. He could have a snooze, watch exactly what he wanted on his TV, finish the blood cleaning, and then stroll into the kitchen for lunch. It became an adventure, and Dad loved adventure. He started to laugh more.

One day, the phone rang and a melodic voice on the other end— Gwen, who we'd get to know well—asked, "Is tomorrow good to start? We have an opening, and you three can come in then."

"Us three? You mean us two. Susan and me."

"No, you are bringing your dad. We'll be doing dialysis on him. He'll get his treatment at the learning center. And you and your sister will be his techs."

This scared the hell out of me.

"Wait, we're learning on Dad?"

"It's not exactly that but close. Just come in, let's start."

Gwen was light, friendly, and matter-of-fact. And my dad's eyes lit up when he heard that our first class was coming up.

Susan was prepared. But I was nervous about entering this unknown medical miracle. We'd spent three years taking Dad to two dialysis centers, going to treatment among the people who moaned and yelled, the man across the room who couldn't keep his breakfast down, and the lady next to us who bled from her needles like a red oil well gushing from her arm. The nurses and techs were overworked, underpaid, and underappreciated. The industrial machines themselves worked hard without so much as a thank-you. We were saying goodbye to all of them and entering our own private sanctuary.

But could I really do this? Cannulate my father, insert the two paramount needles into his skin, and regulate and facilitate a machine that complicated? My father and sister were much more enthusiastic; they discussed it incessantly, with me quiet, watching, my eyes big as saucers.

Dad was up extra early the first day of training. My dad, with the military mind of an engineer, was either on time or early. I used to be late constantly, but eventually I learned that time is money, currency, people's lives. You waste their time by being late; you waste their lives. With my dad's dialysis and his health challenges, I knew that more than ever. I was through with being late. Time was too precious for that.

Susan came into the living room, fresh and ready. She looked excited. Dad stood, his green military jacket and his veterans cap on, his walker in front of him. My mom had a forced but bright smile on her face, watching the man of her dreams accepting yet another call to duty.

The private learning facility was near the football stadium. Dad was in command: pointing out the right exit and telling Susan where to make a left and where to park. There was an elevator at the facility, but Dad wanted to take the stairs. The stairs! Going ever so slowly, we took the stairs: Dad was hanging on one arm, the walker was in my other, and Susan brought up the rear with a duffle bag full of food and supplies for the day. We made it up and through the automatic doors and found our seats by the receptionist. I could tell that Dad was enjoying the unknown, everything new and freighted with possibility. Susan filled out some forms while I sat with my arms around Dad. Not so much for him, but for me.

"You've got to learn how to wash your hands."

I recognized Gwen's voice from our phone call. Our teacher came out into the reception area, limping from a bone spur in her foot. She guided us over to the sink and spent ten minutes indoctrinating us into the first church of handwashing: the tops, the palms, the thumbs, the nails, then repeat, repeat, and dry. Washing takes more time than you thought. And don't touch anything—*anything*—until you get your gloves on. Only then can you enter the inner sanctum where the private dialyzers are housed.

First, the weigh-in. Dad was a couple kilos over his base. No problem; there was an easy fix. The fluids could be removed. Private style. And then we were ready to begin.

Gwen walked us into his room. It was a good size, with a brand-new chair, a brand-new dialysis machine, and cabinets full of supplies beaming at us with promise. And it was his—and ours—for the next few months. Dad hopped into his chair while Gwen fitted Susan and I into our smocks and masks, working to keep us immaculately sterile. She unpacked the equipment, describing everything as she did it, and quickly set up the dialysis machine. The machine was smaller than we were used to. The tubes and needles were the same, but here the process felt more regimented, Gwen's activities different than what we'd seen from the techs at the dialysis center. And it was private. And quiet.

She moved through the maze of responsibilities at lightning speed. She inserted both needles as if she was pinning a wedding dress—Dad smiled the whole time and said he felt nothing. She described how the machines work—the arterial needle brings the blood to the machine while venous needle brings the blood back to the body—and gave us booklets to study. She told us that this was where we would be every day for three months straight. We could have one or two days off for the weekends, but otherwise, no breaks.

I was quiet for the three hours of dialysis, like it was the first time for me. I watched Dad rest his eyes, saw my sister taking notes, and listened to the hum of the machine and the talk about Gwen's upcoming wedding and the surgery on her bone spur. It all felt so much more normal than dialysis had before. I closed my eyes for a second, and he was done. Gwen unhooked him quickly, and before we knew it, he was back up at the weighing machine.

Before we left, Gwen handed us two rubber tubes and a pack of needles. We needed to practice at home.

"Imagine sticking these needles into your father's fistula. You don't want to blow the vein, to infiltrate it. That's painful. We don't like pain."

She poked a finger at my arm to prove her point.

Dad was a chatterbox the whole car ride home. He felt so special. Private dialysis is a celebrity experience, and my dad had been a celebrity his whole life: as a kid, handsome and winning; as a soldier, strong and popular; and as a dad and husband, celebrated every night when he came back home. This wasn't exactly the sort of attention you wanted, but he was basking in it anyway. It was better than being in a room with twenty others having their blood cleaned, relying on his kids to ask a tech to check the machine. Here we had Gwen, and soon, it would be us.

I sat with the rubber hose after dinner, in the apartment we leased in Scottsdale, slowly inserting the needle, imagining it was my dad's arm. Emily and Gracie watched as the rubber accepted the sharp sixteen-gauge willingly, but I often missed the path. That was infiltration, and not what we wanted. I thought about Gwen poking my arm. "We don't want pain."

My dad sat in his chair at the kitchen table, watching as Susan and I learned how to cannulate. I wished I had the confidence in myself that he had in me.

The supplies were already on the table when we came in for our second day of training. Gwen asked if we'd studied as we washed up and donned the protective equipment.

"You two are setting up the machine," she said.

Time *to* Thank

We were temporarily stunned. The second day? But we took out our books and worked our way, step by step, through setting up the machine. It wasn't hard, but it was complicated and needed to be precise. Then Gwen asked who wanted to cannulate Dad.

"After one night's practice?" I said.

"No time like the present."

Susan threw up her hand to volunteer. Dad was ready—he believed in her. Sue picked up the needle and slowly, steadily put it against Dad's skin. Gwen kept her hand on top, helping to guide her. I was sweating so much my goggles fogged up, and I could barely see. And then, *plop*. The needle was in. It felt like a rocket ship had taken off. There was applause from Gwen and a few of her colleagues who had stopped by the room. By the time I had gotten my goggles off, the second needle was in, the machine up and running, and Dad was settling in for his three-hour ride. Everything was calm. From there, it was our job to maintain and watch the numbers: blood pressure and venous and arterial pressure, while making sure Dad's appearance stayed rosy.

I watched the blood go in and out, and I almost fainted. I'd seen this hundreds of times before, but the fact that we were doing it—that Susan was doing it—was roiling my stomach. I knew that I was next.

I sat up most of the night, just me and my rubber hose. Inserting, removing. I was studying the instructions over and over like it was some obscure bit of Talmud. Sunrise greeted me just as I fell asleep. I'm a guy who doesn't need much shut-eye, so I was up and ready before anyone else. Dad came out, dressed and shaved, looking like a million bucks in the exercise outfit I got from one of Lionel Messi's assistants in Barcelona—he was so proud of it, and it fit him like a glove.

Before we knew it, we were back in the room, washing up, sterilizing, and getting our gear on as my dad sat in his chair. He had his usual cherry lollipop in his mouth, and he stared at me.

"Your turn, son."

I froze. My skin got damp, my mouth dry. I looked at Gwen and my sister. I set up the machine with Gwen assisting me, checking the connections and telling me where I needed to clip in. We sterilized Dad's fistula. Gwen handed me the sixteen-gauge needle. I looked in Dad's eyes. He rolled the lollipop around in his mouth, casually. Smiling. Gwen put the needle in my hands. Susan was watching me like a hawk: this was her dad, her dad's fistula.

And then the needle slipped out of my gloved fingers. Sweat seeped from my pores, through the top of the glove.

"Can I dry my fingers?"

Gwen took my gloves off. I washed and sterilized my hands again. Then the gloves went back on. Dad continued swirling his lollipop. I placed the needle on top of his fistula. It felt like I was learning to fly a plane with my dad in the back. Susan watched, and Gwen watched with her hand on top of mine, guiding the needle into the vein. A quick piece of tape, a small pillow of a cotton ball to keep it in place, and *voila!* It was in.

"Let's do the second one."

And we did. The machine started, and I breathed a sigh of relief so loud that Gwen laughed and shook her head.

"That wasn't so hard, was it?"

"Maybe not for you!"

I don't drink often. But when I brought Dad back to his castle that day, I had a glass of tequila that my brother-in-law had ready in case anyone wanted it. Dad had a quick sip. Against the rules, but it was a big day. Bigger than I'd had in a long time.

Then we started the run. The three of us went to dialysis training every day. Gwen started to spend less and less time in the room. She'd weigh Dad in and let us do the math, figuring out how much fluid needed to be removed. Then we would set up the machine and stick. Dad got used to us doing it. Susan got extremely good at it. I had my issues, but finally became great at it, and we traded turns every other day. Over time, Susan did more of the cannulating—she was the one who would be officially certified, just in case I had to go back to LA for a job or if something came up back home. I became her assistant. We trained for months, and it became second nature. And Dad was happy. This was miles more comfortable—and so much calmer—than the dialysis centers had ever been.

The months went by. Gwen had her bone spur surgery and got married. And then, one Monday, Gwen announced it was time for us to set up a clinic in Mom and Dad's den and have Veterans Affairs give us the supplies we needed. We needed to empty the room so we could fit in the chair, the dialyzer, and the many supplies. It was time to go home.

This scared the bejesus out of me. No more monitoring by Gwen and her colleagues; no backstop; no net. But we were ready. It was time to go home.

The necessary equipment was delivered, and Susan spent all night setting it up. Gwen and her associates came by to make sure everything was ready. And that first day, Dad slept in a little later than he had before. All he had to do was walk from his bedroom to the den, now transformed into a luxury dialysis suite. He had his own TV, his favorite snacks, and the sunshine through the windows. There was a sweet, clean smell; family photos and knickknacks; his familiar bathroom; and a closet full of his clothes and Mom's pocketbooks. All of this added to the ease. From that very first day, it was like we had been doing it for years in the den. It was all Susan, and her husband, Bob, who made his man cave my dad's personal dialysis center. It became friendly, almost inviting. And when we were done, we unhooked him, he weighed in, and then he slowly walked himself to the kitchen. I watched him regroup, get himself back to being Stanley, and then have lunch before a nap. And then on to the rest of his day. No travel. No waiting. No sharing machines, techs, or air.

It was all his.

It was like a well-oiled machine. Susan and I were at his disposal. Mom became a part of it as much as she could. We did the work five or six days a week, every week. We got the fluid in—sometimes with difficulty, but most of the time with the ease that comes from repetition. It became our daily routine. We were used to it. We got good at it.

That was the way it was for one harmonious year. We were lucky. No complications. One infiltration—only one. And nothing to distract us from him. It was Dad, and only Dad.

He liked it that way. And so did we.

"You are not going out in this storm."

It was mid-December in 1973, and all I wanted to do was go watch donkey basketball. This was *the* highlight of my school's winter calendar: the school rented ten donkeys, brought them into the gym, and put on a student-versus-teacher exhibition match with the animals. Lots of donkey poop on the wooden slats, and about as much fun as anything I could imagine.

But it was below thirty-two degrees, and ice was hanging off the aluminum siding of every house on the block. There was a big oak tree a few houses down from ours, and even from my kitchen I could see the way the icicles had formed on it like some magnificent sculpture.

"You're out of your mind," my mother said, washing the dishes after dinner. "It's way too icy for anyone to drive, especially that idiot Bruce Johnson."

But I wanted to go.

"I've spent so many days inside because of you two," I said. "I'm grown up—I can make my own decisions."

"You're fifteen years old," my mother said. "We make your decisions, and this one is you stay in tonight."

"Bruce is a good driver. He's had his permit for months now."

"I work with Norm Johnson," my dad said. "He's a schmuck, and his son is a schmuck. Please don't go out tonight. It's icy."

My dad was pleading with me—that didn't happen very often. But I wouldn't listen.

"I have to go to this, Dad," I said. "I never go anywhere. And it's not even icy."

He put his arms on my shoulder. I could see how much broader his shoulders were than mine.

"Not a smart idea."

But he didn't say no.

Bruce drove over to pick me up, and I ran out with the hood up on my Eskimo jacket, covering up my tight disco slacks and my Huckapoo polyester shirt. The car slid to a stop, and I looked back at the house. My parents were watching from the bay window, shaking their heads with their arms crossed over their chests. I looked up at them and shrugged. The skidding was just a rogue patch of ice—there wasn't going to be any more out there, especially on the plowed roads.

There's a feeling you get when you defy your parents' orders. You know there's a good chance they're right. But you do it anyway.

I got in the car. Cathy and Sharon—Bruce's girlfriend and my non-speaking date, respectively—were already inside the cab. Bruce was a skinny, second-tier tough guy who adopted the ego of his tougher friends. I felt good being close to a cool guy, even if he was more of a shadow of a cool guy than the actual thing. He stepped on the gas, and the car took off. I looked out the rear windshield, my parents watching, not moving, as we drove down the snowy street, past the houses trimmed with jewel-colored Christmas lights. Bruce drove with his arm around Cathy, narrating as he drove and watching Cathy more than the road. We drove under that big, old oak tree with the ice dancing on every branch. It wasn't that far from the school. What could go wrong?

My sister Judi answered the phone.

"Get Mom please," I said.

"Steven?" she said. "What's wrong?"

"Nothing. Get Mom."

"Mom! Steven's on the phone—something's wrong."

"Nothing's wrong," I said. "I just want to talk to Mom."

I heard the extension pick up.

"Steven, what's wrong? Where are you?"

"Mom," I said, trying to maintain my indignant attitude. "Nothing's wrong."

My father got on the phone. He talked to me, calm and slow.

"What's going on? Where are you?"

"Dad, everything is fine."

"Where are you?"

"I'm in the emergency room at Massapequa General, but I'm fine."

My mother grabbed the phone back.

"You're fine? You're in the hospital, and you're fine? I'm going to kill you. Stanley, I'm going to kill him. *We told you not to go out!*"

"Mom…"

"Don't give me that 'Mom' stuff! Stanley, talk to him. I'm going to kill him."

"Steven, are you alright? Why are you in the hospital?"

"We got in a little accident."

I was sitting in one of those rooms with two sheets for walls in the ER. I only had a scratch on my head. Bruce was laid out on a table one sheet over, faking unconsciousness. We were all fine—they'd brought us there as a precaution—but he knew he was going to have his head handed to him by his father. My parents slid the sheet to the side. My father was as cool as a cucumber, and my mother hot as a holiday stove. She started to cry when she saw me. They had already talked to the doctor.

"We walked past Norm Johnson in the waiting room," my father said. "He was bellyaching, 'My boy's unconscious, my little boy.' I told him, 'Norm, you're a schmuck; he's faking it. You and your son are both schmucks.'"

My father had his hands firmly on my shoulders as he told me this. It was in the same way when he was cautioning me about the ice.

We drove home in silence. Both of my sisters kept putting their hands on their throats, the meaning of their gestures clear: I was finished. Done. Kaput.

We walked up the driveway. It was covered in ice, but I was still somehow feeling indignant, even after everything that had happened. Then, as if on cue, I slipped. It seemed to happen in slow motion. My head was headed straight for the concrete—until I felt a huge hand and a steel forearm catch me. Those hands again.

"Not icy, huh, Steven?"

I looked at him.

"Am I a schmuck, Dad?"

He smiled at me, helped me up, and gave me a squeeze.

"You're my son. You are not, and never will be, a schmuck."

The Arizona weather started to change; by November it was cooler in the mornings. I opened the window in my parents' room, thinking the breeze might do some good. I dressed my father and, as I put on his socks, tried to sell him on watching a movie instead of the TV during his treatment. I thought a good comedy, or maybe a Western, could lift his mood. I loaded up the iPad that I bought for him with movies that I thought he might like. But he was adamant that he didn't want to watch.

"But you like the Tom Selleck Western," I tried. I felt completely asinine.

He cried out to the ceiling and put his head in his hands. He just didn't feel well. He was tired and hurting. He asked me for Tylenol.

Susan was usually in charge of the medications, but she had a doctor's appointment that day. She had her own health issues, a blood disease that had her clotting too quickly. The veins in her legs needed to be opened with syringes twice a year, a painful endeavor. I could see all this weighing on her—she had resigned from her job as a reading teacher for first graders, giving herself over entirely to the pressure of caring for our parents on top of her role as a wife and mother. She was on the clock every day starting at five in the morning; I noticed how early she went to sleep most nights. It was a full-time job, taking care of seniors. But they had earned the care—they sure gave it to us.

I was in charge that day. I went as quickly as I could to the medicine cabinet in the kitchen. I saw a bottle marked Tylenol and shook out two red pills. I filled his measuring cup with just a smidge of water and dropped in the straw that he had to use for all his fluids. My mother walked in just as he downed one of the red pills.

"Steven, that's not for him," she said. "He gets the regular. Oh, Stanley, give me that other pill."

"Why?" my father said. "I want Tylenol. I need Tylenol."

"These aren't for you, Stanley. Steven, his Tylenol is in his drawer."

I had given him extra strength. That was a mistake. I saw it on the shelf and, going quickly, just grabbed it, wanting to ease his pain. But I looked again, and there in his drawer was a plastic Tylenol container marked "Poppy."

I was trying so hard, every moment. But I was making mistakes more often than usual. Dad was getting worse, and I was tired. But I was beginning to really loathe myself for those mistakes.

There was the day my father told me he never wanted to talk to me again. His wealth manager at Morgan Stanley had been fired without notice, leaving his clients in the lurch. I had contacted one of my trusted stockbrokers and had him talk to Mom. Dad was furious when he found out. He said I was no longer his friend, and that he would never talk to me again.

It cut me deeply. My father's words had always been my beacon. I knew he was having issues mentally, but it made my shoulders sag anyway. It didn't matter that I knew a lot of it was coming from the pain and angst of dialysis. Even though I knew he wasn't himself, those words still hurt.

Friendships used to come so easily.

In 1982, I was twenty-two, and I knew it all. I was popular, and I was sure it was all real and legit.

"Friendships are like flowers," my dad said. "You have to water them. Or don't have them, like me."

My dad was always candid about his priorities. But me? I had loads of people I called friends. All of us single guys, banging the gong starting Wednesday—who was up for the weekend? Our group had power and charisma, the eight of us up-and-comers making any table we sat at come alive with laughter and secrets. It didn't matter if we were at nightclubs or fast-food joints, house parties or back-yard pools.

But the years faded like old photographs. And as I got older, it was more and more about accomplishments and money. As men aged, that seemed to be where friendships grew. Being a good person was nice, but the real question was: "What have you done for me lately?"

I got to see this firsthand. It was 1995, and I was having lunch with my agent. He was a cold prick. A friendly-looking man came over to our table, excited and breathy.

"Hey, Mike, I've been calling you. Almost a dozen times. And you didn't call back."

"Yeah, you idiot. Get the picture?"

He turned his head back to me and continued the diatribe he'd been on before. The man slunk off, backwards, stunned by the disdain and embarrassment. And the worst part was I knew that if he was making money, he would have been welcomed.

"The guy doesn't make a cent for the agency," the agent said. "We're getting rid of him."

How the hell could the world be so cold?

Another one of my father's favorite sayings: "Laugh, and the world laughs with you. Cry, and you cry alone."

It had been swirling around in my brain since I was a kid. For a long time, I didn't want to accept it. But it has proven to be so true. The older I get, the more I start to notice just how true it is. Show business is like life, except exponentially more so.

It didn't matter that I had, in my own way, scaled the mountain of show business and done better than most who'd put on the crampons and begun the climb. Back when my footprints were all over those slopes, I got lots of phone calls, invitations to everything, and freebies. But as my business line quieted, especially as I spent more and more time in Arizona, my social calendar got smaller. The "friends" didn't call as often. More calls outgoing than incoming. And the red Bat Phone failed to light up as often as it once had.

"The world is transactional," my dad used to say. "It has no reflection on you as a person. You can be the nicest guy in the world—it doesn't matter. But a murderer who can make other people money? The world will seduce you."

There's a saying that friends have their time. And acquaintances even less.

But the older I got, the more those little moments of connection mattered to me.

I was in New York, auditioning for *Death of a Salesman* with Dustin Hoffman. I came pretty close to getting it, but ultimately they went with John Malkovich and Stephen Lang to play the sons. I felt let down—I really thought I was a contender. So, my manager, Keith Addis—a smart and savvy man—invited me to a dinner he was having. He promised me that it would help assuage my disappointment. That didn't seem possible, but I figured it was worth a try.

I pulled up early, and the maître d' showed me to the table. I thought I'd be the first one there. But as I was led across the stylish dining room to the center table, seated there already was my manager. Next to him was Trudie Styler, and sitting next to her was Sting. And then, from behind me, I heard a voice I recognized.

"I thought I would be the first to arrive. We're fifteen minutes early."

It was Tom Cruise, and his then-wife, Mimi Rogers. They hustled to their seats. And there I was, next to Tom Cruise and across from Sting.

Keith winked at me—maybe this would help distract me from losing my role in *Salesman*? And he was right. The evening was a delight, with this lively and friendly group of artists getting to know one another. Sting was especially a class man, interested in all our thoughts. Tom was a funny and energetic dinner guest. The ladies were beautiful and full of their own stories. I couldn't believe it. Here we were—music icons, movies stars—all with our own desires, insecurities, and creativity. We were just people, striving for that one elusive thing: happiness. The chance to close our eyes at night and be content.

We all rose in unison at the end of the night. The air was a perfect Manhattan crisp, and we grabbed cabs—no limos here.

When my dad called the next morning, bright and early, I told him that I'd met Sting the night before.

"Who?"

"You know, the famous singer? Sting? From the band?"

"I don't know who Sting is. Is that his real name?"

"No, Dad, but he's a big deal. I was at dinner with my manager, and he and his wife joined us."

"What's his wife's name?"

"Trudie."

"Well, that's a normal name. It seems like you might have made some friends."

I laughed.

"Dad, I think it was just a chance meeting."

"Yes," he said, "But the experience will live on, way past your recollection."

And it did.

My mom and dad were in the Mayo Clinic at the same time but were only able to see each other a couple of times. Here is their reunion.

Our eighty-ninth birthday party for Dad. Singing telegrams, Cajun cuisine, and being together.

Chapter SIXTEEN

The freeways in Arizona are fast. There are daredevils out here on these wide and well-maintained highways. I see a motorcycle doing wheelies—the guy must be going ninety miles per hour.

Ninety. That's my father's number. He uses ninety like a mantra. He talks about it at every meal, tells it to every person he comes in contact with. "I'm turning eighty-nine this year, but I'll be ninety next year—ninety!"

The farms along the freeway are full and ready to be harvested. I look out at the expanse, the fruit ripe and plump and waiting to be picked, the corn high. This land in the middle of the desert is alive and rich, a paradox made possible by water, and plenty of it. This bounty, this basket full of life, will be reaped. And then the fields will be empty. I wish I didn't see everything like this these days. I shudder at the parallel.

It's time to say goodbye to the 10, my faithful companion since all the way back when it called itself the Santa Monica Freeway. I drive by the old racetrack on the corner of the 10 and the 303. The building was torn down three years ago, but I used to drive my car through a hole in the gate, stop and wonder about all the lives that passed through here—the joyful wins and the ruinous losses, people seized by gambling fever, the promise of gold bullion. It was an old wooden structure—it still had cotton candy stands that looked straight out of the '50s and decades of old tickets littered in bunches in the dust. But time goes by—my time, and my dad's time, the most precious time that I'm a witness of.

I'm on the 303 now, driving by the same stores and warehouses that once gave me that new feeling when I first came to Arizona from New York. Back then, even a Dick's Sporting Goods sign gave me a feeling of adventure. Now I watch them go by, and my head is heavy. I hope every day that Dad feels better. I forget on purpose that he's on dialysis. I forget on purpose that he's not himself anymore.

I pull off at the exit to Lone Mountain Parkway. Why the hell did they name it that? Such a lonely mountain. I'm getting close now. I'm almost there.

The gates to the country club development, where my family lives, are open wide. It gives my dad so much happiness every time we go to the restaurant at the club. He talks with everyone, tells his stories, and then moves on to the next booth. What a chatterbox he is. Full of optimism and laughter, hope and care. Remembering what other people once said to him, even if he can't hear them in full anymore. I think about his strong legs and big back, his arms two bags of muscles, and his smile. His smile is like no one else's. I light up every time I see it.

I make a left, drive down to the spot where I lose cell phone reception every time, and then another left onto their block. I look at the houses of the neighbors, at the stop sign that stands sentry, urging me to come to a full stop and grimly watching those who ignore it and speed on by. Here's the park where my dad loved to bring the dog, Rudy, for a walk.

I make a wide turn, so I'm parking out of the way of my brother-in-law Bob's car. I get out finally, feeling the tightness of my legs after so many miles on the road. I have a little superstition about not walking around the back of my car, so I make sure to walk around the front on my way to the house. I get that from my mom and my grandma—we come from a long line of superstitious people. The drapes of the house are open, and I go to look in my parents' window. I see my mom fluttering around the room, getting ready. I say hi, and she laughs and tells me I'm a creep for looking in windows. I smile at her and then continue onto the garage. I like to go in that way, instead of the front door, keying in the code and letting myself in. I remember first coming here, back when Dad was up and at 'em. I was different back then too. I didn't know what lay ahead of me, the journey my father would take, and that I would be by his side, helping him to walk.

The garage door opens. I go into the house. I feel a momentary pang, missing the days when Dad would hear my car and come out front to greet me with a smile. But I'll see that smile soon enough. We're here to celebrate his eighty-ninth birthday.

I wake up the next morning with my heart pounding. I can feel the rhythm beneath my skin. I swing my feet out of bed, wishing my father could do the same. He wants to be ninety so badly. His eighty-ninth birthday is the overture. Next year will be the full show.

I walk down the hall to my parents' room. The air conditioning is on, the flaps on the ceiling unit waving back and forth in greeting. My dad is asleep on his back, his expression relaxed.

"Dad," I say quietly. "Are you up?"

His dark eyes open with a flutter, and then a lightning bolt of a smile. He has been awake for hours, waiting for the chance to begin his celebration.

"I'm up," he says quietly, trying not to wake my sleeping mother. "It's my birthday today." He says it as if he was ten years old.

Slowly he peels back his colorful blanket, revealing the Brooks Brothers pajamas that covers his thin, lithe body. He swings his feet to the floor with a bang.

"That was pretty great!" I say. "You're in good shape."

"Wait 'til I'm ninety—I'll be in even better shape."

In the bathroom, he leans on the counter and looks at his face in the mirror. I can tell the wrinkles bother him, but he ignores them for now and begins his morning routine: toothbrush, razor, a quick wash of the face. He motions for his striped bathrobe, and I get it for him.

He shuffles down the hall and obliges when I ask him to pick up his feet—his doctor recommended that he does this to keep his muscles in good order.

His face lights up when we round the corner, and he sees the balloons and the banner, everything we could muster to make the day feel special. But this isn't even his party, just the preamble.

He stands and waits as I run to disconnect his oxygen from the bedroom device and switch him over to the living room machine. Susan is getting his breakfast prepared: hard-boiled eggs, black coffee, cream of wheat, and a Boost protein drink—he calls it "Boot." And the *Wall Street Journal*—he loves the *Journal*, loves the stocks and bonds that he manages with an adept hand. He's the one who told me to get out of the market in 1987, 2000, and 2008. He's the one who told me what to buy, who to listen to, and who to ignore. And he's the one who loves me so much that, between bites of breakfast, he takes my head in his hands and kisses me. I am one of his accomplishments, living proof of his teachings, carrying on his name.

My wife, Emily, comes into the kitchen and hugs him. Then Bob, up for hours already, gives him a warm embrace. Finally, my mother enters the kitchen with her usual casual greeting and colorful jokes. She kisses his head, and I can tell between breaths that she's hurting. Her love, her husband is in a hard place, and she shares every difficult moment with him. I close my eyes and try to see them both as young and vibrant, walking with abandon. I imagine them laughing loudly, giving each other the hugs and passionate kisses of youth. Today they are cheek to cheek for what seems like hours, still holding hands.

"Happy birthday, Harry," she says. That was my grandfather's name, but my mom loves to call my dad Harry.

A hummingbird lands on a leaf outside the kitchen window. My dad looks over at it.

"That's your mother, Ann," he says. "It's Katie."

He looks at my mother for a long time. I wonder what he's thinking about. Is he musing over my Gram Katie's spirit, or thinking about the hummingbird, still lingering by the flower outside the window?

"Come on, Harry," my mother says after a time, squeezing his palm. "Let's get breakfast over and start the day."

After breakfast, my dad smiles like a little kid caught with a secret.

"I'm going to get back in bed for a few minutes. Just a little cat nap."

My father loves—*loves*—to sleep. He tells me that when he goes to bed, he forgets everything: the things that don't work, the disappointments, the grudges. He would always wake up refreshed, ready to forget whatever argument he had with my mother or one of us kids the night before. It is one of his superpowers. I watch my dad snuggle into the covers, pulling them up to his chin. My mother keeps the air conditioning at sixty-eight, and ever since my dad's triple bypass, he's run cold.

We have reservations that afternoon for a private room at Pappadeaux, a Cajun restaurant my dad loves. This is during Covid, so taking Dad out is chancy, but I'm hoping the private room will make things safer. We've bought tons of decorations and trinkets: Mardi Gras beads, a "You Are Number One" banner, necklaces, poppers—any kind of toy that might make the table more fun.

And for weeks, I have been working on a singing telegram. Not easy to find in Phoenix, but I do: Happy Entertainment. A kind and generous company that not only humors my instructions but also embraces them. There has to be singing, but not sexy, so as not to offend the ladies. The singer must know "Earth Angel" by the Penguins. And they have just the person: Flo. Isn't it ironic—her name is Flo, and his kidney is all about flow.

Dad gets up from his nap in time to field a few celebratory phone calls: from my sister Judi in Jersey, a few lifelong friends, friends of Susan's, and friends of mine, all calling to wish him well. Some he wants to talk to, some he doesn't. He has less energy these days, and he's sleeping more and more. I know the naps are good for him, but I don't like that he needs them and what it means about where things are going. But he still has these spurts of energy. When they ask him to walk across the room in physical therapy, he runs his walker with every ounce of his ability. It gets a big laugh, and it shows that, G-d damn it, he's still got it. He's still "Stan the Man." Still Stanley.

Dad wants to shower before the party. I help him out of his pajamas and get a clean towel. His body is an even thinner version of how I remember him, and I weep inside. I take off my own shirt and help him into the shower.

My mother watches as he dresses. There's sadness in her eyes, but I see a twinkle when my dad cracks a joke about me putting his socks on. He's wearing a snappy pair of athletic pants and a checkered shirt with his soft and supple Armani Eisenhower jacket. He asks me to get his hat, the veteran one in black with the gold star on the front. We connect his portable oxygen concentrator and head out.

The whole family squeezes into one car: my mother and father, Susan, Bob, and their daughter Carly, and Emily and I. The whole ride over I'm thinking about the singing telegram. I can't wait for him to see it. The owner has told me that Flo is ready with his favorite song, the one that he and my mother listened to as they first fell in love: "Earth Angel."

The restaurant is lively when we arrive, the crowd active amid the sound of the New Orleans music, and the bar full. The maître d' knows it's Dad's birthday and has the private room ready. I snuck over earlier in the day, while Dad was sleeping, and decorated the room with banners and tchotchkes. I tried to make it look as festive and inviting as I could.

Dad strides through the crowd. It's his day. His eighty-ninth. People stop him to say hi and to thank him for his service—they respect the military immensely in Arizona. My dad loves to hear it. He brings people close, holds their arm, and tells them a story. One of his favorites: about the future wife with whom he traded love letters, SWAK—sealed with a kiss.

Time *to* Thank

It takes nearly twenty minutes to get him through his adoring fans and into the private party room. His eyes dance as he walks in, still holding his walker, and his mouth drops in surprise. The room looks like a carnival: ribbons, beads, and banners, all dancing against his black-as-coal peepers.

"I can't believe it," he says over and over. "I can't believe it."

We bring him to the head of the table. Waiters and waitresses flood the room, masked up and paying homage to the man who gave his service to his country, his love to his family, and his devotion to his wife. And then the food comes, like a scene from some legendary Arabian feast—except here it's all Cajun. A mountain of shrimp and crawfish, bowls built for giants filled with gumbo, and jambalaya fit for a king. And it was fit for a king: our king.

"Dig in!" Dad hollers, and the celebration begins in earnest. The music roars: jazz, trumpets, trombones. It feels like we're on a carousel, standing in the center as the colors and music swirl around us. I think that's why Dad loves this restaurant so much, the way it enriches all the senses. He is alive, breathing deeply, eating everything that he shouldn't on his renal diet. But this is a day of forgetting: forgetting the no-nos, forgetting the difficult recent past, forgetting the future, forgetting what we can or should or will be. We just *are*. And it is bliss.

The room is full of laughter and conversation. And this—the family all together—is his greatest accomplishment. Sure, being an Airborne Ranger is something, along with his two degrees in electrical engineering and accounting (the last of which he received from Lynn University at the age of sixty-five), his time as an NYPD officer—uniform and plainclothes—and his career as an executive at the vanguard of the electronics industries. But being a husband, father, grandfather, father-in-law, and uncle—that's what makes him the proudest. This is his legacy. His trophy case. This is his everlasting tribute to his own mother and father. To himself. To us.

A door opens. A brightly colored sheet of fabric walks in, and then we see arms, legs, a shock of red hair, and lipstick.

"Time to party!" announces Flo. The singing telegram is here.

She has a waiter bring in her music box; it sounds like an organ when it plays. She is vibrant and charming and gives Dad every bit of love and enthusiasm in her soul. He is the star of the day, and she treats him as such. Mom has no issue with Flo falling in love with Dad.

"Stanley," she says. "I want to tell you a story."

She then proceeds to tell us all the tale of little Stanley Jerome, from Forty-Fifth Street in Boro Park, who was born in an apartment, not a hospital; who learned to work on a farm in the summers next to his dear, smart, loving mother; and who watched her translate immigrants' letters into English in her apartment. She gave him his first vitamins and started him on the nutritional journey he would be on for the rest of his life. Flo tells of the Stanley who learned to lift weights, becoming the physical specimen that boys admired and girls swooned over, of the Stanley who went to City College, of the Stanley who served his country. We hear about the Stanley who married Ann, who became Dad, and then Poppi.

And then "Earth Angel" fills the room. The Penguins music comes over us like a waft of perfume, a warm breeze, a mist of potent red wine. Mom stands and kisses her man, and Dad stands too and sways to the music, to their song. He pushes his walker away, and the two of them dance like it's 1954, when they first started dating, when they fell in love. The applause afterwards is like we were in Madison Square Garden. The room is filled with every waiter, busboy, bartender, hostess, and car valet that Pappadeaux employs. Some are crying. Some are laughing. Most are wishing they had love like that: sixty-five years of marriage, seventy-five years of love. I watch from my seat; my eyes glaze over with the sweetness that fills the air. No one, no one, has ever had a better birthday.

Dad turns his head to me and mouths "thank you." He repeats it to Emily and Susan. He turns to his wife, takes the oxygen ring out of his nose, and tosses it aside. And then he kisses my mother like they're in the living room of their first apartment. *Flash.* Just hold this image, this feeling, forever.

I take out my phone to record a video of my dad. Something I already know I'm going to cherish forever. I ask him to tell me about his birthday.

"I was so surprised," he says. "This was beyond all my thinking. You made my birthday unbelievable for me."

A few seconds go by. And then he looks at me.

"What will it be for the ninetieth?"

We all laugh. Suggestions start flying around the table. Someone offers a nightclub.

"We will be on a boat!" my dad says. "A yacht!"

More happy laughter. I look over at my mother and promise her we'll make sure the boat is docked. If Dad wants a boat, he'll have a boat. But really, all he wants is to make it to that number. To ninety.

My dad didn't like his walker. It was a constant struggle to get him to use it.

"Please, Dad," I pleaded whenever I saw him without it. "Use your walker. Please. Every day. Everywhere you go."

"But I don't need it."

"I know, but it's just a precaution. The physical therapist says you need to use it."

He shook his head every time I said that. I knew he didn't want that damn walker. He wanted to walk, fast, on his own. He wanted to run. He wanted to not shuffle his feet. He wanted to go back to the gym, back to bench-pressing almost two hundred pounds. He wanted to chat with everyone in the weight section, buying coffee before and after every lift, and usually getting a free cup because he was so handsome and sincere. He walked without his walker quite often, despite our pleas. He did a little dance as he stole moments away from the metal contraption that announced to the world that he needed help. It didn't matter that it was the top of the line. He didn't care for it.

I get a call at four in the morning. It is May 13. Eight months after my dad's birthday. I'm back in LA. I pick up the phone, and it's my sister Susan.

"Come, Steven. Dad fell."

He had gotten out of bed at two in the morning and decided not to use his metal albatross. It was only twenty feet. But his feet hit the wave in the carpet, and he fell on his hip, breaking his pelvis. The pain—the devastating pain of it.

I drive from LA to the hospital. Because of Covid, I can't get in. I beg—plead—with the president of HonorHealth, the system that runs the hospital. I am allowed to try and comfort my dad. But no pain medicine they give him is working. The pain is excruciating. And with the pain comes delirium as they feed him ever stronger drugs to try and find some relief. His mind is being poisoned as his body is numbed. These are terrible days.

We come home after twenty days to a hospital bed we set up at home and his La-Z-Boy recliner. I hold his hand. My mother, sister, and wife all sit around his bed. We watch his chest not rise—watch his eyes not open. And every time, I plead with G-d for him to come back. And he does.

We had done at-home dialysis for a year. We had hundreds of thousands of dollars of dialysis equipment from the VA. Dad doesn't like it—who would?—but he never misses a session. He shows up. Every time.

But now, my mother says that it is time. I can tell that the decision to take him off dialysis is a stomach-wrenching one for her.

"No, Mom, please," I say. "Let's keep doing it."

My mom looks at me with her bright green eyes. A faraway look today. Even though my mother is shorter than me, I can feel her looking down at me. I'm the one who can't stand up, can't be at my tallest. Can't this son accept what is? The decision has been made, and I'm trying to stop a freight train.

"No, Ma," I try again. "He'll come back. Please. Let's just try. Please—Sue, Mom, let's keep doing the dialysis. It'll work."

"It won't, Steven," she says. "It's not helping anymore."

It is July 11. The hospice nurse has told us that she thought my dad only had a few days left. He wasn't talking, wasn't eating, wasn't drinking. His breathing had slowed to a gurgle over the last few days. I sit with him constantly. My wife, Emily, comes to relieve me and rub his feet so I can take a break every few hours. That moment alone gives me the illusion that everything is fine. I know it isn't. But I ignore it. My hero—my rock—my wisdom—isn't opening his eyes. But I still think that, somehow, he is going to come back.

Susan has the talk with him earlier in the day. I hear her talking to him.

"Dad," she says. "It's okay. You can go."

When she leaves the room, I hold my dad's hands.

"Don't go," I whisper to him. "Stay. Stay."

It's later in the day now. We're moving my father to sit upright in the La-Z-Boy. He has a habit of slipping down, which is uncomfortable for him. Every few minutes Susan or I pull him back up. But this time, his eyes are closed.

"He's okay," I insist. "He's going to come back."

I will not accept that the tips of his fingers are gray. I ignore that it's one of the signs the nurses have told us to look for. No. I rub his fingers, massage them, trying to get the blood flowing again.

"You are going to be okay," I say. "I'll get the blood back into your fingers. I'll get you back, Dad."

My sister looks at me with sadness, watching this pathetic character—me—go through his motions. I talk to Dad. I hold his hand. I kiss him. Whisper to him.

I can't accept it. The room is quiet, and I can't see the angels there. I don't want to. A rabbi told me that the brain doesn't accept death right away—it would be too painful.

"What?" my sister says. "Steven, what? What's going on?"

My hand is holding his forearm over his dialysis fistula to feel the thrill. My father's thrill was strong every day, a "Ruffles have Ridges" kind of a pulse. But now my hand can feel only the weakest pulse. I have never not felt it pulsing like a stream full in spring after the snowmelt. I look at him, put my face next to his, and listen for his breath. Do I hear nothing? I put my ear closer until it's touching his face.

"What, Steven, what?" my sister says again. Susan has a look on her face. Fear. The closest I can think is when she was still small—the seven-year-old with a skinned knee, the kid who thought there was a boogie man in the room, or the look she gave when she thought she had no friends, which was the end of the world then. Her face flashes disbelief at me, even though for days she has told me she knew it was coming.

"I don't know," I say. "I don't know."

The nurse who has been sitting in the back of the room takes her stethoscope now and comes over, feeling for his heart.

"No." Reluctantly, she looks at us. "He's gone."

What? What do those words mean? No. No.

"Come back!" I yell at him. "Come back, Dad, come back!"

I start doing CPR. I push on his heart. Yelling at him the whole time to come back. My sister leaves the room. I'm screaming now.

"Don't go, Dad. Please. Please!"

My mother comes in with a bewildered look, one that I understand and don't at the same time. Her brow is furrowed like I've never seen before. She sits next to him, on the other side of me. She strokes his forehead.

"Oh, Stanley. Oh, honey."

I watch as she softens, her bright green eyes clouding over. She kisses him.

My sister runs in, very upset, bringing Emily. Susan is shaking as she moves close to him. My father. Her father. Mom's husband and love. My wife's father-in-law. He lays there, his mouth slightly open and his eyes closed. They say you see a look of peace when someone passes. I don't. I see him not wanting to go. He left reluctantly. He was the lion. He is the lion. So we hold onto him. I keep yelling. Asking him. Pleading.

"Come back, Dad. Please come back."

I sit with him as the nurse checks him and writes down the time. 10:00 p.m. No, no. Please don't write that. Please, Dad. Please, *please* come back.

A heavy air sits in the room. We are quiet. Susan is sobbing. Tears are running down my face. Emily holds his hand. My mother strokes his face. We hear each other breathing. I look at my mother—I can't take my eyes off her. *Please look at me, Mom. Please make him come back.* She could always make everything better. She could always get my dad out of a mood. Always make him laugh. Make him change his mind. Make him smile and acquiesce. I watch as she sighs, saying again, "Oh, Stanley. Oh, Stanley."

And then she says what I don't want to hear.

"He's with his mother now," she says. "His sister, his family. He's with his best friend, Marty."

She looks at me when she says "mother." My father loved his mother with every inch of his heart. She was a kind, smart, beautiful lady. She was the only one in the family who believed in him, who knew he would become somebody.

The nurse says quietly that she is going to call the mortuary. We sit there for what feels like forever. My mother asks us to leave the room.

"I want a few minutes with my husband."

We all walk out into the hallway. Staring at each other. I hug my sister. I hug my wife. Then I let go and stare at the floor. I look at the door of my parents' bedroom, open just a crack. My eyes are heavy, and my mouth waters. It waters, like my eyes.

The nurse comes into the hallway. "The mortuary is on their way, but it'll be three hours."

"Three hours?" my sister whispers.

The door to the den opens, and my mother walks out.

"I'm going to sit in the kitchen."

I watch as she slowly walks away, rounding the corner to the kitchen. The three of us—Susan, Emily, and I—go back into the den.

Dad hasn't moved. He's just lying there. His eyelids are softly closed. And his hand—the one I held for hours while we watched *Seinfeld* or looked at the painting of Italy above the TV—is still. The movement has just stopped. Like that. Like nothing.

When a person has a cold, they get better. A broken leg eventually mends, and they walk again. When someone has a migraine—like my dad used to get—it goes away. He would come out of the bedroom afterwards, smiling. "Smiling Jack" we called him. But he isn't going to get up now. He isn't going to open his eyes to me. He isn't going to hold my hand or kiss me and tell me how much he loves me. He just isn't.

But I still don't believe it.

"Dad," I say again. "Please come back, Dad. Please."

My voice trails off. I hold him, I hug him, and I cry. I cry deeper than I ever have before. And he isn't around to hold me and tell me, "It's all right, Steven. Stop it. It's going to be okay."

Twenty years ago, my father had a triple bypass operation. Mom and I were standing outside their home in Florida while my father lay in bed, his first night home from the hospital. He was sleeping, and we walked outside to get some air. I looked at my mom's bright eyes and she held me with both hands. Time was slow.

"You're going to have to be strong," she told me. "One day…"

I knew what she was saying. But I didn't accept it. No one's leaving me. I shook my head as if I understood, but I didn't. My parents won't die. Please, G-d.

But now the mortuary is hours away. The rest of my family is in the kitchen. I hang my head in the heavy air and hear only my breathing.

My father made all the decisions for us. He was the voice of reason. His voice chimed in last always, like a sturdy and reliable timepiece. I'm sure my mother doesn't remember that conversation late at night in the humid Floridian air. Or maybe she does. Maybe I was the one who forgot. Because I didn't want this to happen. I didn't want him to go. Push the thought away and ignore the voice that has been whispering to me, for some time now, "He's tired, Steven. He doesn't like how he's been living." I've argued against that voice out of my own selfishness because I can't live without my father. He's going to get better. He's going to get up.

When I look up, my mother is in the doorway. She looks at me, looks at Dad, closes her eyes, and sighs. Slowly, she walks in, sits on the other side of me, and holds his other hand. He is warm but getting cooler. His cap is still on his head—his Korean Veteran hat. Now, both Mom and I are breathing. It's the only sound. My father's eighty-ninth year.

These seconds are so precious. Never have they been dearer. It's like we are on the moon, without time or gravity, or even thought. We are just so small. Next to such a large man.

Dad forever told me everything will work out, "You've got to believe in yourself, Steven, no matter what anyone says."

I look up to my father. Every day, I remember
his lessons and speak to him in prayer. He still
gives me tips on life.

Epilogue

We had started planning for the funeral a couple of years earlier. My sister and I shook our heads the entire time at how morbid it all felt. Now I think: of course it was morbid. That was the point. But it was a help that my parents did it. They had already picked out their plots, under a tree in the cemetery.

People came from everywhere. They came, they cooked, they bartended. They sent mementos, food, love and care. The fridges were full; so were the counters and the shelves. They were there for us.

I remember the eulogies and the casket. I asked to see him twice—to be close once again. I put a note into his hands. We carried him into the hearse and then to the plot. I saw a John Deere digger waiting on a hillside. It was hot as anything; we waved fans. A flag was folded and placed over his casket. In the distance, there were four soldiers. When the colonel indicated that it was time, they performed a twenty-one-gun salute: three rifles, seven shots each.

The crowd got to their cars quickly afterwards. I stayed last. I put my hand on the box. I wanted to put some of me in there so that he wouldn't be alone. And then we went home, to a house overflowing with friends. I walked out front to talk with a buddy and get my breath back.

The first month, my friend Liam sent a star named after Dad. Al sent food. Mike and Steve and about a hundred other friends showed up. They gave us honorary plantings for Dad in Israel. Sweets and booze and calls and notes. Love—that's what they gave me. All of it love.

I said Kaddish. I got a grief counselor. Mary has been a great source of gentle comfort. She educated me on the dark-suited grief. Grief has a way with you. It hits you on the side of your head. And in your eyes. And your heart. I hear "Earth Angel" and start to feel my heart in my throat. My breathing gets faster, shallower, my mouth gets dry, and I feel a crush in my chest.

It was a surprise to me that I could just keep getting up and functioning when the grief was freshest. I think the shock was a shield for me as I kept going. I had things to do, but with my eyes sad and at half-mast. I thought grief would be more of an involuntary response. But no: it was new and complicated, and I had a great deal to grapple with.

I still have a hard time when I see a video of my dad or hear a clip of my parents singing "Earth Angel." I weep—it just hits me. A few people close to me have said that this brings them down. But I just still have him with me.

I'm happy and so grateful that I had my life with my dad. But for me, it was too short. I would have liked an eternity with my dad. He was that kind of guy. He had a long, good life—it just wasn't enough for this son.

After about eight months, my mother told me that she wanted my dad's stuff out of her rooms. She had lost her man, her guy, her everything. The other side of the bed empty when she reached for him in the night. But it was time. We revamped their part of the house in Arizona—their room and the room where we had been doing Dad's home dialysis, where we spent so much time caring for him. I kept many of his trinkets. His clothes are in my closet: his hats, the ties my mother gave him. I wear one of his jackets all the time now—and two of his shirts. I keep his handkerchiefs in my pocket. He was from the school that every gentleman should have a handkerchief with him. So I do too.

It's been a year now. A rubbery, slushy year. I walk differently; I think my gait has a missing skip in it. Maybe I'm more aware, more observant. At the same time, Dad's influence on me is more apparent every day. I'll see a photo of myself and, for a second, I think it's him. I see my head nodding like he did; I listen in a more focused way. I've started peppering my conversations with the word "occur." That's Dad.

I listen to his voice messages almost every day. He was something else. The real thing. He listened when you spoke—really listened, reacted, and wasn't thinking about his own agenda. He was old school—built on principles. I see other sons with their dads, and I feel that hole in my chest, that cold wind on my neck. I remember how lightly he touched my arms, my face. I miss my mentor, my sounding board, my net. Now I worry about hitting the pavement. But I do believe he's here, and he set things up to move me through the world. I do believe that.

It's gotten less intense, as the months go by, but my grief is still very present. The melancholy in me just won't leave. He stays hanging on the doorposts of my heart; he sits on the gate with a sly yet understanding smile.

I miss his gentle reminder that nothing is too serious. I need to hear that. I tend to take everything seriously, and Dad often said, "Steven, don't take things to heart." Dad was a guy who said look ahead, move forward, but I was the one who put the brakes on. I've forever been a worrier, and sometimes I do forget to enjoy. But only now do I believe I have to try to do that—to be happy, to enjoy life. I've had my father's words hit me when I was leaving my dressing room to shoot a scene. I stopped and thought, *Yes. I have to remember my lines, my moves, my actions—but* enjoy *it, Steven. Enjoy it*. For the first time in a long while, I did just that.

I've had dreams about my dad. One in particular. I am in the kitchen with Emily and my nephew Danny. I hear a noise in the hall. I go to look and when I turn, I see my father. He is healthy and tan, smiling and barefoot in a shirt and shorts. "Dad! Dad!" I can't believe my eyes.

Even in my dream, I think he's a ghost. I ask if I can hug him, thinking it will just be air. But I *feel* him: the warmth of his chest, the kiss on my head. I bring him out to say hi to Emily and Danny, to prove he is there. He comes into the kitchen and waves to everyone before going back into the hall. And I wake up.

It's hard for my mom to go see Dad. I find it a comfort. So I go often. I talk to him and tell him I miss him. I can't explain yet what it is. But I feel better going to the cemetery, standing before his plot beneath the tree.

His passing has had a profound effect on me. I feel like it's a new chapter. I do feel that he's with me. And laughing. Tan, cool, and in excellent shape. Pushing me ahead.

It's not over, the pain that hits me when I think of my dad. Maybe it'll never be over. But I do get that feeling, coming to the surface more readily now, that I have to live my life. I want to live a life my dad would be proud of. I want to be the guy he brags about to everyone in heaven; to be the man my ancestors can smile at; the man my family and friends are proud of. I want to stand up, hold on to the reins, and build my life; to make him laugh up above and tell everyone, "That's my son."

Every one of us is in the caregiving world. Emily gave me this quote attributable to Rosalynn Carter. Mrs. Carter says there are only four types of people on this Earth:

The first is a caregiver.

The second will be a caregiver.

The third was a caregiver.

The fourth shall need a caregiver.

We, every single one of us, will be playing a part in this journey.

My favorite photo of Dad—his laughter when we gave him a cool sports car, as fast as the wind, for his eightieth birthday. He drove it with a smile every day. "Here's my tip, my son: Enjoy life."

Acknowledgments

Acknowledgments are more than thank-yous. They have a special meaning.

First, I want to acknowledge my family and my father's care team. There are many ways to care for someone that you truly love. We chose to give ourselves in person, to be by my dad's side as much as possible:

To my mother, the center of Dad's love, his wife, partner, lover, and the keeper of his laughs. Daily we would see them holding hands; it was the signature of their relationship. Sixty-five years of marriage, sleeping next to each other, laughing together, depending upon each other. They are and shall forever be one person.

To my wife Emily, who gave Dad her love, spent much time at his side, and supported me through this journey. Your love gave me room to be there for Dad.

To my sisters Susan and Judi, who cared with all their hearts. Susan was the light that shone in Dad's face twenty-four hours a day and, by the by, could run a dialysis machine like no one else.

To my brother-in-law Bob, who carried Dad through, literally and emotionally, went to the ER without hesitation, and gave me the hugs I needed at the right times.

To my niece Carly, who gave Poppy her heart every day, and he was brighter because of her.

To niece and nephews Danny, Jenny, and Jack, who made Dad light up whenever they spent time together.

To Jill and Al Segel, who are family, supporting my endeavor, and Al brainstormed the title, *Time to Thank*. My appreciation is infinite.

To Joe Pappalardo, my brother who is forever there for me. To the caregivers who were our colleagues in holding Dad through the long nights:

To Dr. Robey, our vanguard, who gave of herself personally and professionally. Her attention and care gave Dad such love.

To the doctors and nurses at the Mayo Clinic, HonorHealth, and everywhere Dad received love and attention.

To the Hospice of the Valley, who were there when decisions had to be made.

With this book, I intend to tell the story of how family, friends, and caregivers chose, together, to be an army of care. An army of love. For the man who gave us his everything. Thank you to everyone who played a part in that coordination of love.

I also wanted to acknowledge the people who gave me room to run when I began to think about telling my story—who allowed me to talk limitlessly about this portion of my life, to figure out the right way to communicate this story, and helped me use my eraser to get the manuscript right.

To Jake Steinfeld, who in the aisle of a grocery store told me that my story was a book. And that my drive to Arizona, and my father's journey, was something that everyone could benefit from hearing.

To Jan Miller, who became my literary agent after a call from Jake, telling her in no uncertain language that he believed in this tale. And Jan listened to me with her heart, spent hours upon hours talking with me, and encouraged me to start to write. She promised she would find the right publisher, and she did.

To Spencer Gaffney, my editor, with whom I learned to write with control and meaning, who was firm with me and allowed me to walk my own path through the literary woods too.

Time *to* Thank

To Gretchen Young, who took up Jan's call to be creative allies, who read my writing and agreed that there was a book in that mountain of pages, and that she would work with me and publish it.

To Anthony Ziccardi, whose optimism and understanding, along with his own connection to his father, gave me such blue sky to fly my words to those I want to reach.

To Maddie Sturgeon, whose patience and infinite ability to listen allowed me to try this and that, and that and this, till the cows came home.

To Rebecca Silensky Echols, a comrade devoted to getting the details right and giving me her opinion immediately when asked.

To Judy and Sean Katz, who gave me their love and empathy, listening to me when I called needing to talk.

To the many close friends, and you know who you are. You've listened to me countless hours and gave advice and I appreciate every moment of it.

To my dad, who would stare at me with those dark understanding eyes, and let me be myself, let me be with him when he told me to go. Let me hold him when it was me who needed holding. Let me make mistakes. Who read almost every page of this book, kissed my cheek, and gave me opportunities to step up and grow.

I love you—that's forever.